THE SMILE THAT HIDES
THE PAIN WITHIN

SECELIA TOLBERT

Secelia Tolbert

DEDICATION

To my children, April & Michael, the trial and tribulations that we have endured over the years, has nothing over the joy and happiness that we found. I would not change a thing, if it meant that you two would not be a part of my life. I never knew what true love was until I had you.

To my grandchildren, my heart is smiling because of each one of you. The world has no idea what's in store for them because of your future accomplishments. Trinity - International Superstar, Joslyn - Gymnast, Mikeala - Ballerina, Major - Football Player, & Milan -??? (still to be seen). Never give up and don't be afraid to try new things.

To my sisters and brothers, thank you all for loving me unconditionally

and

To my mother, may you now have peace.

ACKNOWLEDGEMENT

I would like to thank Amber Moses for helping me with my first published creation. With all that she has on her plate, she took the time to say, yes, I'll help you. Only a true friend would do this for you. And thanks to her mom Donna and Gizmo for lending her to me.

I love you guys,

SeCe

The Smile that Hides the Pain Within

PREFACE

This is the story of my trials and tribulations of raising two beautiful children as a single parent. As I walked the path that God has chosen for me, I cried at times, I laughed often, I prayed for help, and I cried some more. The journey was hard and painful, but rewarding and joyful all at the same time. I found myself uplifting other people in my struggle and realized that no matter what was thrown at me, I always kept a smile on my face. My mission was to raise my children and provide for them the best that I could with what I had and in the meantime, help them to be the best productive adults in this cruel and mean world of ours. My smile was a gift that God gave me as part of my armor, but it took me a great many years into my adult life to realize that fact. My life was a struggle from Jump Street when I was born with red spots all over my body. I was allergic to almost every food on the planet, but I had to eat to live while eating was making me sick. I was even allergic to grass, so going outside was painful. As a very energetic child, wanting to do nothing but run and play, I had to stay in the house and watch the other children having fun outside. I've been raped, stalked, hit by a transfer truck, fought cancer off not once but twice, I have had two homes foreclosed, and had cars reposed, but through it all still I smiled. I've always felt that God would not have given me this journey if He did not have a plan for me. God would not put more on me than I could bare. God gives us tests for our testimony. The question I now ask myself and others, "Why not me?" THIS IS MY TESTIMONY

"YOUR TEST IS YOUR TESTIMONY"

Secelia Tolbert

CHAPTERS

Secelia Tolbert

YOU CAN NOT BE
WHO YOU ARE GOING TO BE
AND WHO YOU USED TO BE
AT THE SAME TIME

SECELIA TOLBERT

IF YOU WANT TO BE HAPPY, YOU HAVE TO BE HAPPY ON PURPOSE, WHEN YOU WAKE UP, YOU CAN NOT WAIT TO SEE WHAT KIND OF DAY YOU'LL HAVE.
YOU HAVE TO DECIDE WHAT KIND OF DAY YOU'LL HAVE.

JOEL OLSTEEN

FIVE STEPS OF FINDING HAPPINESS

1. OWN YOUR OWN HAPPINESS: BE RESPONSIBLE FOR YOUR HAPPINESS
2. CHALLENGE YOUR STORY: WRITE YOUR STORY AND IF YOU ARE NOT HAPPY WITH THE WAY THE SCRIPT IS GOING, CHANGE IT.
3. ENJOY THE JOURNEY NOT THE DESTINATION: THERE IS JOY IN THE PROCESS OF THE JOURNEY.
4. MAKE RELATIONSHIPS COUNT: WITH GOD, WITH YOUR SPOUSE, WITH YOUR CHILDREN & FAMILY, BUT MOSTLY WITH YOURSELF.
5. BALANCE WORK AND PLAY: IF YOU WORK HARD; THEN PLAY HARD.

IT IS NOT WHAT YOU LEAVE YOUR CHILDREN,
BUT WHAT YOU LEAVE IN THEM!

BISHOP TD JAKES

WE NEED OUR YOUTH TO SUCCEED IN THE FUTURE.
WE MUST INVEST IN OUR FUTURE.
THEREFORE, WE MUST INVEST IN OUR YOUTH.

Secelia Tolbert

HEAVENLY FATHER,
YOU KNOW EVERY DECISION I NEED TO MAKE & EVERY CHALLENGE I
must FACE.
PLEASE FORGIVE ME FOR THE TIMES THAT I TRY TO FIGURE THIS LIFE
OUT ON MY OWN.
I NEED YOU. I NEED YOUR HOLY SPIRIT TO GIVE ME STRENGTH,
WISDOM, & DIRECTION. AMEN.

UPLIFTING ENTERTAINMENT

DON'T JUDGE.
YOU DON'T KNOW WHAT KIND OF STORMS SOMEONE JUST WALKED THROUGH.

KRISTEN BUTLER

Secelia Tolbert

YOU ARE TOO BEAUTIFUL TO BE BELITTLED,
TOO BRAVE TO BE BEATEN &
TOO BLESSED TO BE BROKEN.

MARCUS GILL

BEAUTIFUL

THINGS

HAPPEN

WHEN

YOU

DISTANCE

YOURSELF

FROM

NEGATIVITY.

THE SECRET

NEVER LOSE SLEEP OVER SOMETHING THAT ISN'T WORTH STAYING AWAKE FOR.

SPIRIT SCIENCE

YOU ARE RESPONSIBLE FOR YOUR LIFE.
YOU CANNOT KEEP BLAMING SOMEBODY ELSE FOR YOUR
DISFUNCTION.
LIFE IS ABOUT MOVING ON.

SECELIA TOLBERT

I AM NO LONGER ACCEPTING THE
THINGS I CANNOT CHANGE.
I AM CHANGING THE THINGS
I CANNOT ACCEPT.

MICHELLE OBAMA

TO MY CHILDREN...

IF I HAD TO CHOOSE BETWEEN LOVING YOU AND BREATHING...

I WOULD USE MY LAST BREATH TO TELL YOU

I LOVE YOU

UNKNOWN

Secelia Tolbert

THREE THINGS YOU CAN CONTROL
YOUR ATTITUDE,
YOUR PREPARATION,
&
THE EFFORT YOU PUT IN

MIKE TOLBERT II

YOUR SMILE IS YOUR LOGO

YOUR PERSONALITY IS YOUR BUSINESS CARD

HOW YOU LEAVE OTHERS

FEELING AFTER AN INTERACTION

BECOMES YOUR TRADEMARK

JAY DANZIE

OH, MY LORD, I'M HERE

It is February 7, 2016, and I just arrived. I am at 4900 Marie P. DeBartolo Way, Santa Clara, CA. Home of the San Francisco 49ERS, Levi Stadium. You see, my son is playing for the Carolina Panthers, one of the two teams playing today in SUPER BOWL 50. Yes, that is right you heard me correctly, MY SON IS PLAYING IN SUPER BOWL Y'ALL. As the families unload from the buses and get our instructions on what we need to do and when to return to the buses after the game, I sit in awe and wonder, "Lord, Thank You; we made it." I am listening to words being said, but I do not hear anything. Other people are laughing and talking, but I am in another world. I am just smiling, and smiling, and smiling some more. "Lord, God Almighty, we made it."

I have on my new customized smoke gray #35 Carolina Panthers' Jersey; I have all my beads and badges hanging around my neck. In my hand, I have my brand-new camera, which I bought just for this occasion. I have on my new gray Nikes, and I'm feeling just fine. My hair is blowing like crazy, but I'm not worried I have it pinned down pretty good. People are everywhere. A man walking around on stilts, cheerleaders yelling, drumlines beating to the beat, kids running around screaming, and yes, a couple of people already drunk falling and tripping over other people. I can smell all different types of food being cooked, BBQ, bratwurst, hamburgers, hot dogs, french fries, pretzels, popcorn. Oh my, God, there is food everywhere. All of this even before we get into the stadium. People have tents set up and tailgating, drinking and having fun. Everyone that can be seen is having a great time.

There are so many orange Denver jerseys walking around here. Where are the blue Panther jerseys? We need our fan base today, more than ever. Roaring Riot, where you at? On every corner there is someone in a yellow shirt guiding us and directing us in the right direction. I'm so thankful for their assistance. We are shown where to go to make it through security. Man, it's worse than going through security at the airport. I think I need a cigarette after all of this patting down and stuff. How many times are they going to ask me for my ticket? I have shown this damn thing twenty times, I think. Glad I have it hanging around my neck. Finally, we are in the stadium and headed in the direction of our seats. Wait a minute! Is that Braylon Beam being interviewed over there? Yes, it is. I run over to get my big hug from him and his parents. Braylon is being interviewed on the Ellen DeGeneres Show, and I just ran in the middle of the taping. Oops! "Braylon, introduce us to your friend," says the reporter. "This is Mama Tolbert; Mike Tolbert #35's Mama," Braylon yelled with that big toothless smile. I love that kid. We get to chat for a minute with Ellen's crew and then move on to find our seats. Up the stairs and to the right ma'am, I am instructed finally. But wait, is that the bathroom? Let's do that first. Is this a bathroom at a football stadium? This is enormous and clean. I see you Levi Stadium; you did this right. No one has to wait in line ever with bathrooms this size. Okay, okay, I'm done talking about the bathroom. I thought the bathrooms at Bank of America Stadium were nice, I mean really nice.

My daughter and her two girls are sitting with me in section 132. We are right behind the goal post on the Panthers' side. There are thirty-two of us here to support my baby, but our tickets are all separated. There are not that many people inside in their seats yet; I guess because it is three hours early. Come on you all know me, I arrive early to all of the games. I have to make sure my baby is focused and ready to leave it on the field. Trinity, my oldest granddaughter, and I walk down the stairs to field level to talk to Mike, when he comes out to warm up. "I LOVE YOU, DO WHAT YOU DO." I've told him this before every game for over twenty years. Then we hug and kiss on the cheek, and IT'S GAME TIME!

Let me introduce myself. My name is Secelia Jarlarice Tolbert. I am the third child of Shirley Walker and the fourth of seven of Willie G. Walker, Jr. I am one of eighteen grandchildren by Rance and Addie Foster, and I really don't know how many by Willie, Sr. and Essie Walker. The mother of two, April D. and W. Michael II. Mother-In-Law to my son's soulmate, thank God we love each other too, Shianette. Grammy to four of the most beautiful, intelligent, sassy, and loving grandbabies, Trinity, Joslyn, Mikeala, and Major. Also, the Grammy to three grand dogs, Tyson, Layla, and Peanut. After a failed marriage, I became a single mother left to raise two of the most beautiful children a parent could pray to God for. The struggle was real, times were hard sometimes, but together we survived.

Life has a way of throwing lemons at you sometimes and then there are times when you can take those lemons and make lemonade, sit back, relax, and enjoy the peace. As a parent, it was my responsibility to raise my children to be productive adults in society. However, as a single mother, it sometimes was so hard that I felt like giving up and throwing in the towel. Nobody ever told me it would be this hard to raise a family. Growing up you see all the shows on TV, and everything is all roses, but REAL LIFE IS NOTHING LIKE THAT! Married with children, the little house on the hill with the white picket fence, two point five children, the perfect career, driving the family car on yearly vacations, and everyone is happy and healthy; are some of the things that I dreamed of as a little girl. Oh yeah, I was supposed to be married to Randy Jackson, Michael's little brother and my sister was going to marry Michael. DOES GOD HAVE JOKES OR WHAT?

My father left, my mother and I did not get along, my grandmother hated me, I had health issues, and a failed marriage are the things that I had to deal with. I would ask the question all the time, "Why Me?" Why did it seem that no matter what I did, something was always going wrong? I would try and do the right thing, and something happens. Do something, that if my family found out, I would be disowned and got whipped for real. Go to church, pay my tithes, go to work, take care of my children, and my home is foreclosed. Pray and study the word, attend Bible Study and Sunday School, but then have to deal with cancer. "Lord, Why Me?" Get raped and stalked, get robbed, and hit by an eighteen wheeler, "What have I done wrong, to deserve this life?" My husband's girlfriend tells me, he's hers, and I find out that he has another son, three days older than my daughter, "Is this what life is about?" Something has to shake, life is not supposed to be this hard. But what am I to do to change it? How am I going to change my life? One of the biggest problems is that I was in denial. I never thought I had a rough life. Sure, there were times that I cried, but you know what, THAT'S LIFE!!!!!!! Nobody ever promised us a Rose Garden. We go through things, we have difficult times in life. Each situation makes us stronger. We have choices in life and with those choices comes consequences. Good choice, good consequence and bad choice, bad consequence. The consequences that I have endured in life are the results of the decisions that I have made in my life. I did not listen to my gut, my heart at times. I did not hear God other times. I perceive my life as having chapters. Once something is done with, the chapter is over, and I turn the page and continue on to the next chapter. Some chapters are long and hard, unbearable to read while the next chapter may be tranquil and I find myself laughing through the pages. But whatever is going on, I have to stay positive and believe, "THIS TOO SHALL PASS!"

I can choose to be sad, have a bad attitude, and hate everything and everyone in my life. Or I can choose to be happy, be positive, and simply love life no matter what life has to offer. It takes just as much energy to be unhappy as it does to be happy, so why not choose to be happy? Why not be grateful for the things in your life, the people in your life, the place that your life is in now? Remember the saying, "I complained about the shoes I had to wear until I saw the man with no feet." We can stay in a funk and complain, we can be negative and never explore the positive side of life, or we can remove the haze over our eyes and live life to the fullest. I CHOSE THE LATTER, TO LIVE LIFE TO THE FULLEST. I call it putting on your big girl panties, pulling them up and let's go. If life throws an obstacle at you, dodge it, tackle it, block it, or merely move around it and put your big girl panties on and GO!

How else can anyone explain the chapters of my life? Like I said, "Thank you, Lord, we made it!" Instead of saying, "Why Me?". I'm saying, "Why not Me?"

AS LONG AS I HAVE LIFE,
I WILL SMILE!
LIFE IS A GIFT AND
IT IS PRECIOUS!

TRACY RANKINS

**IF GOD BRINGS YOU TO IT,
HE WILL BRING YOU
THROUGH IT.**

SUBURBIANS 3:9

EARLY YEARS

I was born as the third child to affluent African American parents in Atlanta, Georgia in 1962. My parents had it all during the middle of the Civil Rights Movement. My father happened to be the first Black Foreman for Mead Packing Company, one of the largest paper manufacturers in the country. My mother was a jack of all trades. She worked at The Rustian Company and made personalized stuffed toy animals. She also had her cosmetologist license and did hair as a side job, which means someone was always in our house on the weekend getting their hair done.

My mom was the typical woman of the sixty's. She cooked, cleaned, worked, and got her ass beat by my dad. She had broken bones, and blackened eyes, but she never stopped doing what she was supposed to do. It was the man's job to take out the trash, cut the grass, and keep the cars clean. While it was the woman's job to do everything else, it did not matter that she was working forty plus hours outside of the house also. My brother, the man-child in the household, was taught by my father to have the same values and rules as he. My sister and I were taught to learn how to do the woman's job.

As the baby girl of the bunch, I was my daddy's baby. He actually claimed me as his child and I could get anything I wanted from him. Yes, I was spoiled rotten by my dad, and I think my mother resented the relationship that my daddy and I had. Let's remember, I was the youngest of the group. All I know is that my dad gave me everything. I think I gave being spoiled a new name as I grew older. I could tell my dad that my brother was hitting me or sitting on me or just doing something to me, and my brother would get a whooping. I could ask my dad to go somewhere like the fair and we would go. I could just say; I want and I had. I never knew the problem I was causing until later in life. I did not know that my father did not think that my brother was his child because my mom got pregnant before they were married. Never mind that they looked just alike. I didn't understand when my father said my sister was too black to be his child. Again, we all look just alike. My dad and his siblings were so different in skin tones that you would think they came from different parents, but again they all looked just alike.

My father's gene line also gave me a skin disease called eczema. I could not get a mild form that only breaks me out when I come in contact with something that I was allergic to. I had to have one of the worse cases and I had inflamed puss bumps all over my body except my face. My brother also had eczema, but he could receive shots that controlled his eczema. The inflammation bumps on my skin would run puss and drain on my clothes so bad that my clothes would stick to the sores when it dried up. I itched so bad that I created ways to scratch. I could stand in the middle of the floor on one foot and scratch my other leg with the other foot. I remember crying one night because I was itching so bad that I told my mama, I wished I would just die. My mother said to me later in life that was one of her unhappier days of her life. To know that your child is in so much pain and agony, and there is nothing that you can do to help them is a pain only a parent can feel. I remember going to so many doctors when I was growing up. One doctor said, soak in water. Another one told me to stay out of the water; it will dry out your skin. Take showers, not baths, and only stay in the shower for seconds, only take two baths a week. I had one doctor to tell me I was allergic to grass and the sun, which meant I could not go outside and play. I was told that I was allergic to all citrus fruits, all nuts, chocolate, tomatoes, ketchup, and figs had the biggest effect on me more than any other food. My mom had fig trees that had to be cut down, and she had to make sure there were no figs in any of my food.

I've seen other family members with the same skin disease. I even had one uncle that had it so bad but was not doing the things it took to control the disease. My Uncle Clifford's eczema had gotten so bad that he had patches of skin missing where he would scratch so much that he would dig holes in his body. One day we got a call that he was killed in a car wreck. I overheard my parents speaking about how Uncle Clifford lost control of his car because he was scratching. His hands were found digging into his skin on his face. I always wondered if he figured a way out from the pain of eczema. That was the day that I decided that I must fix this problem myself. Yes, at a very young age, not even ten yet, I knew I had to do something for myself.

My mother would hear about a different doctor and she would make an appointment so we could try something new. At one time, I lost track of all the different solutions to my skin problem so we began writing down what each different doctor would suggest. Until one day a family friend came to visit us and told my mother about Dr. Berman in Columbus, Georgia. Dr. Berman was an old white man that stood bent over and he looked out of the top of his inch-thick glasses. He looked like he should have retired thirty years ago, Columbus was a two hour ride from our home, but that did not matter to my mother. She made the appointment and we headed to Columbus. One good thing about Dr. Berman was that he was open on Saturday mornings for patients that had to work during the week. Dr. Berman did his initial consultation and told my mother and me what no other doctor had ever said. First, he explained the disease and why I had it. He said that the disease was in my blood line and that it is only passed through the male gene. This explained why no one on my mother's side of the family had the skin rash, only my father's family. Next, he told us that although I was allergic to almost every food item out there, he said to eat what I want. He felt that if I only ate what I was not allergic too, I would starve to death. I could no longer wear fingernail polish because it was one of the reasons that I continue to break out. Scratching with the polish on was another way to spread the rash to other parts of my body. I could go swimming and run outside; I could play on the grass, and I could take long hot baths again. Dr. Berman's belief was that I had to want to do things to get better and by feeling depressed and upset because of all the things I could not do, it was not going to help me to get better. He wanted to work on the disease from the inside out. Yes, water would dry my skin out. Yes, I was still allergic to grass. However, there was a way to treat my issue and for me to live a stress-free life at the same time. The one thing that Dr. Berman said that I would defiantly not be able to do was to take birth control pills. He stated that one ingredient in the medicine would break me out so bad that the guy I was planning on being with would never want me. However, at thirteen, that was not a problem for me, so I was content.

Dr. Berman started giving me a shot once a month. Since I also had asthma, I could not take the shots more often because the shot would trigger an asthma attack. The choices I had to make, breathe or itch? I was given cream to put on my skin three times per day. The cream was so heavy-duty that there were studies of the cream causing skin cancer, but it worked. I could not use too much because the doctor would only give me enough to last one month at a time. When I took my baths, I had to add Alpha Kerri bath oil into my water for the moisturizing effect on my skin. I always had to wear a cotton shirt and khaki pants or shorts. If I wore a top that had a collar on it, I had to wear cotton handkerchiefs draped over it to prevent the material from touching my skin. The funniest thing that Dr. Berman had me doing is wrapping my arms and legs up at night with plastic cellophane wrap. After I took my bath and put on my skin cream, my mom would wrap me up in plastic every night. I would have to wear white cotton socks on my feet and hands to prevent me from scratching in my sleep. The plastic would help my skin retain the moisture from the bath oil and allow the skin cream to be able to work.

Dealing with the aches and pains of this disease was not even the worst part of my childhood. I was called witches and other names by people that I went to school with. Children can be so mean when they do not understand because they thought they were going to catch what I had. I got into fights with other kids because they were mean to me. Mama would say, just walk away, but I could not figure out where to walk to. No matter where I went, other children would always be cruel and say hurtful words. While living in Atlanta, I was all right because the children from my school grew up with me and they understood what I was going through. They had seen and been through everything with me. They knew when I went to a different doctor and what the new doctor had told me to do. Once we moved to the country, I was in an entirely different environment. The new kids had no idea of what I was dealing with, but that's a whole other story.

After a couple of years, I finally started to heal. The disease was and will always be in my blood, but I had it under control. No longer did I have puss running down my legs or blood on a shirt from where I had scratched too hard. I could go outside without itching. I could go and play outside in the summer time without breaking out. I could even wear fingernail polish because I was not scratching and spreading eczema all over my body. Eventually, I stopped breaking out all over my body as I had in my early childhood. I now only break out on my face. Go figure. I can tell if I eat too many tomatoes because my face will break out. However, I know how to control my outbreaks now. Alpha Kerri Bath Oil and lotions are my best friends, and Westgard Skin Cream will always be in my medicine cabinet. Dr. Berman passed away a few years ago, but he was also a teaching professor. He taught other doctors the practice of dermatology. I found one of his students, Dr. Thomas Lamb, in Carrollton after his death. I no longer need a Dermatologist since my General Practitioner will prescribe any medicine I need for my skin.

As a child, I did not understand what was going on with my body, and why I was infected with this skin disease. The older I got, the more I understood my situation and what I had to do to control this eczema that was in me. It was a part of who I was, who I am, and who I will be. Only death could change this fact. Although my mother and the many different doctors had done all that they could do, there is nothing that anyone can do to completely heal me. Dr. Berman gave me the best advice, and I could apply his advice to more than just medical issues. I could let eczema get the best of me or I could choose to take control. My disease did not define who I was and it didn't stop me from smiling and enjoying life. If I wanted to run outside, drop down in the grass and roll around, damn it, do it! Get up real quick, run and take a shower, but roll in that grass and have fun! Life is too short not to enjoy the time we have here on earth. One thing is for certain, "From the time we take our first breath of life, we start to die." I MADE A CHOICE TO LIVE!

Secelia Tolbert

**LAY THE
FOUNDATION
FOR YOUR
CHILDREN.
BE THE
FOUNDATION
FOR YOUR
CHILDREN.**

Unknown

THE DIVORCE

In 1972, I was nine years old when my mother decided that she had enough. She was no longer going to take the ass whippings that she was getting. She was not going to be cheated on by my father, or mentally abused by the man that had sworn to love, honor, and cherish her until death does them part.

My father was the son of a Baptist preacher and he could have women shouting as he prayed during Sunday morning praise worship. My father was the man that other men looked up to. My father was a deacon of the church and he was a womanizer. My father was an abuser and an adulterer. Other women would call my mom and ask her if she knew where her husband was. They would then laugh and say "oh I know, he is here with me". Women of the church would date and sleep with my father, the deacon, while at the same time they would sit next to my mother on Sunday morning. How my mom put up with it for fourteen years is beyond my comprehension of life.

One thing about my father is that he always worked third shift, so he slept during the day. We always had to be quiet in the house so we would not wake him up. I guess working at night freed him up to go and see his women during the day while we were at school and my mother was at work. Everyone that knew him knew he slept during the day. One time when the Atlanta Fair was in town; my sister and brother wanted to go. Well, of course, I could get daddy to take us. So, they had me to wake him up and ask to go to the fair. And of course, he said yes. We were to get dressed, and he was going to take us to the fair. We were so excited because Daddy never took us to places like this. We went to church and school. Any fun place we went with our mother. As we were driving to the fair, we saw this lady walking down the street holding a little girl's hand. Daddy stopped to ask her if she needed a ride and she told us that she was taking her daughter to the fair. I was eight years old and didn't have any idea of what was going on. This lady and her child accepted the ride to the fair, but they stayed with us the entire time we were there. When daddy bought us something to eat or drink, he also bought them something too. He ended up taking them home after our trip to the fair. Later in life, I realized that the woman my father married after my parent's divorce was the same lady from the fair and her daughter became my sister.

One day my mother came home with a gun and she put it up on the back of the closet in her bedroom. The fights that my parents had started to become more frequent than normal, but they were different. My mom was no longer quiet; she was arguing back. She was yelling and voicing her opinion. She had had enough. This one particular night, my mom went into the bedroom where daddy was sleeping and the fighting began. Where my mom never would hit back, she was whipping his ass. Man, she was giving him a run for his money. She was tossing him around the bed and kicking him; she was another beast to reckon with, and daddy had no idea what to do. My sister, brother and I were standing in the doorway, not knowing what to do. Mama started shouting at my brother, to get her gun and my daddy was yelling, get my pants. He was asleep before the fight, so he only had on his boxer shorts. My sister and I were crying and telling my brother to get Daddy's pants so that he could get out of the house. When Mama went for the gun, Daddy had to run, and run fast he did. Once he got outside, he stopped to look back at us and my Mom had a brick in her hand. We yelled run, but he kept standing there. Again, my Mom was in a different frame of mind and she threw that brick. It went through the back windshield of my Daddy's brand new car. He yelled, my car! We yelled, run!

In the 1970's, the domestic violence law was not enforced as it is today. During that time, men could beat their wives and the police or law enforcers would do nothing about the crime. Later that night after the fight, the police brought my dad back to the house. He never got his pants from my brother, so he had taken a pair of pants off a neighbor's clothesline. The pants were about ten times too big for him. We thought that they were going to arrest my Mother because she had whipped his ass something bad. But, that did not happen. The two police officers asked my mom if she was okay, and she informed them that if he stayed there that night, he would not survive the night. My dad was standing there like he was all big and bad arguing and saying no one was going to make him leave his house. The police officers suggested to my dad that he needed to get some things and they would take him to a friend's house for the night. The police also advised him that coming back to the house without one of them would not be advisable. That was the last night that my father stayed in the house with us.

Throughout the next year, my parents went through a rough divorce. My father claimed that he was not going to pay child support since my mom put him out. He would not continue to pay the mortgage on the house since he could not live in the house. No white man could tell him when he could see his children. My mom was a trooper through the whole ordeal and she went through the divorce like a pro. Yes, we had to move, because she could no longer afford to pay the house note.

With the help of my grandparents, we could move to my mom's hometown of Bowdon, Georgia. Being born in Atlanta and everything that you know, other than a few weekends or maybe one or two weeks during the summer, is city life, so moving to the country was a total life change for all of us. At that age, I could not have had a worse time and hated every minute of being there. I eventually told my mother that she turned us from city slicks to country hicks. Never in my wildest dreams, had I ever wanted to live in the country.

From attending an all-black school to a school where there were only one or two black kids in your entire grade, was more than a culture shock. I had KKK signs marked into my desks at school. I had a teacher once call me a dog, by asking me if I was in heat. We could go to town and see the Klan walking around in full robes and handing out pamphlets to future Klan prospects. I knew that my mom did what she felt was best for us, and there was nothing that any of us could do about it anyways. I remember that the Klan would hold their monthly meetings on the other side of the mountain from where we lived, and we would see them driving up the road to the meetings. I was such a rebellion that I would sit outside and watch as they drove by, my mom would be furious with me and make me come inside. She would say that I should not draw attention to myself or the family, in fear that the Klan would do something to one of us. I had to learn to live in an environment that was not safe for a black person. At school, I had to learn to be friends with people that didn't like me just because I was black. I think this was when I started to grow up and realize that we all are God's children and no matter our skin color, our background, or our religion, we all had to learn to get along and deal with each other.

Out of the three of us, I believe that my sister had the hardest of all. She is and was so smart, that when we moved to the country, she skipped a grade from middle school straight to high school. Not only was she the new kid at school, but she also was the youngest. Where other girls were maturing, and going out on dates, she was still wearing ponytails and plaid shirts. Even with being the youngest, she was the smartest. She could make straight A's and not take a book home. She would not speak to anyone, teachers or other students. She was so quiet that my mother was called to the school because my sister would not speak even if to answer questions during class. My mom thought that was the dumbest thing, out of all the problems that school administrators have at school, you are going to call a parent off their job because their child is not talking. At the same time, that child is a straight A student. At home, my sister would laugh and play with me. She spoke when she needed to, but never would you think that she had a learning disorder. Finally, once the teachers and staff realized that she was listening and knew the material they taught, they left her alone. She found a couple of friends that were nice to her; she joined the marching band, and her high school life was okay. She graduated from high school with honors and went on to West Georgia College, and continued with her Masters in Chemistry at Georgia Tech.

My brother, the oldest of the three had it bad also, but he decided that he would rather work than continue with his education. My brother was the comedian of the bunch. He could make anyone laugh and joke out everybody around. He had another problem with white people; he did not like them. He had a problem with white people, gays, and people of authority. Let's just say he had a problem with everyone. He felt that his way was the only way, and if he said it, it must be so. For years, my brother and I did not speak to each other because I was just as opinionated as he was. My brother started fights with anyone for any reason. He once got to fighting with a man for leaning on his car. He loved fast cars and guns, and many times the two did not mix. At school, he had a problem with the white man telling him what to do and his grades reflected that problem. He once got to fighting with the same white boy three times and the same boy whipped up on him every time.

His biggest problem was that Steve (the white boy), was the one that would walk around in the winter time with no shirt and flip flops. You could find him walking across the roof of the gym on any given day, and he was one of the best football players on the team. I use to say that our players tackled cows in their off time. Steve knew martial arts and was the "Billy Jack" of Bowdon High School. So, this is the person that my brother wanted to fight. When you decide to fight, you need to pick your battles, sometimes it is best just to walk away and all times it is best not to start the fight. After the third fight, my brother was sent home for a week, and he never went back.

Tony, my brother, finally started working with my mom at a local wire company, fell in love, got married, and had his first child. Four wives later, I think that my brother has found the woman that can put up with him. She will not marry him, but I believe that she truly loves him. He once called her by one of his ex-wive's names and she made him write one hundred times I will not call my lady by my ex's name ever again. He had to write the sentences out before she would even take his phone calls. I love that she has softened my big, bad brother.

I found my piece in the country. In elementary school, I met a friend that was a real friend. It helped that she and her sisters were known to be some of the best fighters in the county, which meant I no longer had to fight because the other kids knew we were friends. My grades were excellent, not so much because I was so smart, but mostly because the schools that I attended in Atlanta were more advanced than the schools in the country. The curriculum of fourth grade in Atlanta was the same as the curriculum of fifth grade in Bowdon. My mom was a stickler for education, so we stayed on top of our learning. We would have to read and study during the summers. She made sure that we had encyclopedias and globes for our research. She always wanted us to be advanced and ahead. She believed that an education would help us in life, and since she dropped out of school at sixteen, she never wanted any of us to end up working in factories or cleaning up someone's house for a living. As teenagers, my sister cleaned houses and I babysat. Those jobs were just a means to an end until we could do better and it gave us spending money in our pockets.

Coach and NBA Superstar Dawn Staley once said, "A disciplined person can do anything. Dare to do what you don't want to get what you do want." My Mamma made sure we were disciplined. She could have given up and continued to stay with daddy, but she finally decided she was better than that. Leaving her job, friends, and what she had come to love was hard for her. To become a single parent and raise three children alone was going to be a struggle. But did she have a choice? NO! Would it be better for us to grow up and see the abuse, the anger, the adultery that was happening in our household? NO! Were we better and stronger because she left? YES! Did we miss our daddy in the house? Of course! Was it a hard move for us? You better believe it. Do I blame my mom for not trying harder to make her marriage work? NEVER! The consequence could have been so much worse. What if she stayed? Someone could have died. What if my brother reached the gun before my dad ran out of the house? The foundation that my mother set for us by deciding not to continue to be a battered wife meant so much more to us as we grew older. I have seen and known women personally that chose to stay with the abuser for their children. My opinion on the matter is, get the hell out. Leave as quick as you can. Run and run fast. I know it is not easy, but please don't make the kids the reason you stay. Your children would rather have you alive and happy with them.

Thankfully, my father came back into our lives. I am pretty sure he never apologized to my mother, but he was there for his children and grandchildren. True enough we were grown when this happened, but it happened none the less. Before he passed in 2013, we all had come together as a family. We had to forgive. Forgiveness is not for the offender, it is for you. Being able to forgive is imperative for your own peace of mind. I can forgive you that does not mean I will forget.

THE MOST DANGEROUS ANIMAL IN THE WORLD IS A SMILING WOMAN SITTING IN SILENCE.

UNKNOWN

Secelia Tolbert

IF YOU WANT TO BE THE BEST, STUDY THE BEST.

HORACE THOMPSON

TEENAGE YEARS

As a student in high school, I started to find myself. I became an assistant editor on the yearbook staff and I played basketball. I ran track and made it to state in two different events. I was on the debate team. I was a member of the Pep Squad and let me tell you, we made some noise during football and basketball games. I was a member of the drama team and I hosted a Saturday morning radio show with my cousin James. I played basketball for the Bowdon High Red Devilettes and I was a manager for the boys basketball team until my mother said I could not do basketball anymore. I did not understand that one. I could not play, but I could be a manager for both the boys and girls team. I was a manager for the girls' team, but I was the official scorekeeper for the boys' team. Until this day, I do not know what caused her to not want me play anymore. I was also invited to be in every pageant around. I took second runner-up in the Miss BHS (Bowdon High School) pageant. I was in the Miss West Georgia Fair and I was the second runner-up for Homecoming Queen. However, out of all the things that I was involved in, I was a dancer. I took dance lessons and my dancing helped me with my self-esteem and allowed me to advance in the different pageants. While living with my father, we were not even allowed to play the radio. Once the divorce was final, my mom signed me up for dance lessons and I took dance until the day I found out I was pregnant with my daughter. My senior year in high school, I was offered a dance scholarship to Oberlin University. Once again, my mom stepped in and said no to Oberlin because she did not want me to be that far away from home.

In 1977, I was asked to be a part of the Georgia Close-Up Program. The program is for high school students that were excelling in academics and had an interest in politics. For one week, I could stay in downtown Atlanta and go to the Georgia Capital every day. I could participate in the law-making policies of the Georgia General Assembly. I learned a great deal through this process and met some smart students from all over the state of Georgia. I was scared when my mom first took me to Atlanta, but I eventually figured out that I could communicate with the Senators and Representatives. Speaking with the Governor of Georgia, George Busbee, was a major highlight of the week. We served as Pages for our district Senators, and we were honored with a luncheon on our last day there. Until now, I did not realize how much I love being in charge. Going back to that time of my life, I guess I always had to have my hand in the middle of the pack.

The very next year in 1978, the most exciting thing that happened to me. I was a contestant in the Miss United Teenager Pageant, where I won the talent competition and made it to the next level of the pageant. The loss was heartbreaking, but rewarding all at the same time. Going back home to the small town of Bowdon, I knew that even though I was living in a small town, I did not have a limited frame of mind. I was going to be all right and I was going to make it in life, no matter where I was living.

As I continued my education at Bowdon High School, I was my own person and I strived to keep a straight-A grade point average. Still being a small high school in a small town, I had to deal with the prejudices of the staff and students of the school. Once while sitting in my trigonometry class, my teacher called me a dog, and of course, I went crazy. I guess the city girl in me came out. The problem started because one of my classmates did not have his book for class. The problem was that my teacher gave us two different books to use for the course and every day at the end of class, she would tell us which book to bring to class. Reggie did not bring the right book to class on this one particular day. So he decided to slide his desk over to my desk to share books. He put his arm around my shoulder as we were looking into the book, and the teacher states, "Secelia, if you are in heat, you can leave my room." Heat? Why did she say heat? Only dogs go into heat. My neck snapped back and forth and asked her if she knew what she was saying. Of course, she was defensive with me and said "YES!" She suggested that if I did not correct myself that I could leave her room and go to the office to see the Principal. I got my happy little tail up and marched right out of that room, to see Dr. Westbrook. That was another big mistake. He tells me the story of being a member of the Klan and how in his days, he would spit on colored people and burn crosses in people's yards. This was not going the way it was supposed to. One thing they did not realize or recognize in me was that I was not a quitter. My sister was a student at West Georgia College now, and one of her professors was Newt Gingrich. She told him what happened, my mom got in touch with the NAACP, and it was on from there. Remember when I said I had crosses burned in my yard? This is when it started. I was speaking at churches about what was said to me and how I was supposed to just let it go. By the time I was finished with them, I had an official apology in the local paper and a hand-written apology letter from the teacher and the principal. At my graduation, my principal had the nerve to come to me and tell me that he was glad I was gone. Sorry to tell him but the feeling was mutual.

My basketball coach was also the director of the local parks and recreation department. During the summer and early part of the school year, I would work for him at the recreation department. I kept scores for many softball or baseball games and cleaned up the parks at the end of the day. I even started calling some games when I learned the official rules of softball and baseball. I was also the person that parents brought their children to when they wanted to sign up for different sports and events at the recreation department. I received my first sunburn while working a tournament one summer. Not ever being able to be outside like most kids, I did not know that I needed to put on sunscreen while I was working the tournament. For this tournament, I worked as the official scorekeeper, and I was out in the sun from eight in the morning until well into the night. The first night of the tournament when I went home, I was so burnt I could hardly take a shower. The water stung my skin so bad. My mom had no idea what to do and I ended up calling a friend of mine to ask what I should do to stop the burning. "Cassie, I am burning, and I do not know what to do" after she stopped laughing and crying, she suggested that I get some Noxzema and spread it on the burns. It helped and for the rest of the tournament, I sat under an umbrella to hide me from the sun. The job with the recreation department had its positive points, but it had one great big negative point. I found out what it was like to be stalked for the very first time.

One of the men that worked for the parks and recreation department became attracted to me for some reason. He would always show up where I was working, no matter which park I was working. He always had some perverted remark to say to me. The other kids that worked with me, would laugh it off, but it started to get annoying to me. Being that I was only sixteen years old, he would try to get me to go out with him. I have never been the person to be mean to anyone, and I always had a smile on my face, so I guess he was taking my kindness as a weakness. It got to the point where I had to tell my coach about the advances that were made. Again, I'm here in this small town with my coach telling me that I imagined it and "that white man does not want you," but said he would talk to him. Well, that conversation did not go too good, because now the man was mad at me. His words to me was that he was going to get me one way or the other. My mom made me stop working late hours, because I had to drive home alone. Once I got home, I would be alone for a couple of hours while I waited for my mom and sister to get off work. On a couple of occasions, this pervert would let me know that he knew where I lived and that I went home alone. The more that I tried to stay away from him, he was always there. One night, he started calling me at home and I had no idea where he got my phone number from. He would ask crazy questions like, what did I have on or what color panties did I have on? Sometimes he would just breathe into the phone and not say a word. I would hang up and he would call right back. We didn't have call block back then. My mom had to speak with the coach about the problems that I had. I guess when Shirley spoke, people started to listen. The man was fired from the job. They said it was for other reasons, but we all know why he was let go. I thought everything was fine for a while, but the calls started back and he told me that he was on his way to my house. He knew that my sister was at work until midnight and that my mom was working third shift. I called my mom and my sister. Both took off and came home. The biggest problem was that he lived in Bowdon which was five minutes away. Mmy sister and mother worked in Carrollton which was twenty-five minutes away. I guess I should have been afraid of this jerk, but I had my granddaddy's shotgun and my mom's 22. By the time my sister pulled up in the driveway, I was rocking in the rocking chair with the shotgun across my lap and the 22 lying on the seat beside me. Yes, I knew how to shoot and shoot very well. I had only practiced on cans and milk jugs, but I am sure I would have used his head for target practice. My sister knew that I had a love for guns, so she got out of the car yelling, "Laura (my nickname) it is me, don't shoot." Once she got in the house, we laughed until we saw car lights coming up in the yard and it was not my mother. The car turned around and there is no way for me to know if it was him or not. I am not sure if he came and left when he saw my sister's car or if it was someone else just turning around in our driveway. We lived in the country, way out in the middle of nowhere, and there were only one or two houses. It's hard to imagine someone being lost that far out. However, I never heard from him again after that night.

My teenage years did not get any better after that. I did not have to deal with that jerk anymore, but there were others that were just as bad or should I say worse. My junior year in high school, I sang in our church choir. One of the perks of singing in church choirs is traveling to different church singings. My Mother joined a church in the country after we moved. I never did and I kept my membership at our previous church in Atlanta. The pastor of my mother's church had a son that was on the high school football team and he also sang in a gospel quartet. We started to date and he was the very first boy that my mom would let come to my house. She would let me double date with my sister and her boyfriend. We would be everywhere together and did not even live in the same town or state for that matter. He would pick me up after school or work, he would bring me home after singing, we went to each other's banquets, and I went to his senior prom. He was supposed to be my ever after. He was a year older than me. On his graduation night; my mom, sister, and I went to his graduation. I worked and saved money to buy him a very nice watch for his gift and I was so proud of myself for saving my money for my man. This was the first night that my mom was going to let me go out alone on a date. She did not even give me a curfew time. When he asked her what time, I had to be home, she said for us to be careful and just don't make it too late. I was on cloud nine. We were supposed to be going to a graduation party that some friends of his were having. I did not care if I was with my man. My mom and sister left for home, we got in his Volkswagen and left for the party. We drove and drove, and we never made it to the party. I asked him where the party was and he told me it was at a friend of his house on the lake. I did not know any better and thought that his friend must live way out. We ended up on a dirt road out in the dark somewhere and he pulled off the road. All I saw was darkness and stars. There were no street signs, no lights, no houses, nothing. I stupidly thought he must have run out of gas and asked what was wrong. He tells me that he wants his graduation gift and I laughingly told him that he had it on his arm. He gave me this look and was like, "no, my graduation gift." Truthfully before this night, I had been playing and doing some things with him that I had no business doing. There was a little touchy feely here and there, but I had never gone all the way with him. Well, this was his night and he was not going to have it any other way. He told me I could either get out and walk or give it up. I had been leading him on for a year, so tonight he was going to get what he wanted. My choices were to be raped by the man that I thought cared about me or get out and walk in the dark on a dirt road in Alabama in 1979. As I laid there crying in the passenger seat of a Volkswagen, giving up my virginity, I started to hate this person who moments before had meant the world to me. When he finished with me, he asked me to marry him. At that time, all I could do was hope to get back home and never see him again. He did take me back, all at the same time he was talking to me like we just had the best time of our lives. He thought I was good even as I was asking him not to do this and that I was not ready to go all the way. I told him I loved him, but I was not prepared for the next step. In my mind, as a sixteen year old, I felt like it was my fault. I knew it was not. I should have a say so in what was happening to my body. To be threatened and taken advantage of was a real sign that this boy did not love me. How dare he think I would marry him after this? He better be glad that I could not get to the shotgun without waking up my mother.

Once we got to my house, I got out; slammed the car door and walked away from what I had thought was going to be my future. My entire personality changed that one night. My mother did not understand that I wanted nothing else to do with this boy and all I told her was that we broke up. When he would call, or come over, I would not speak to him. My mother tried to make me talk to him because what man would come crying to get back with a woman? I would never find another man to love me like that, she thought. I did not care and didn't want anything else to do with him. On one particular day, he showed up at my house and talked with my mother. He told her that after he had proposed to me, I broke up with him. He told her that he loved me and that he wanted her to help me understand how much he loved me. She made me go outside and talk to him. She said that if I did not talk to him, I would be grounded and she would take my car from me. When I got outside, he stood there crying all red eyed and snotty noise. I hated him more then than I did the night he raped me. How dare he stand there crying, when I was the one he hurt? That day, I think I learned how to be a professional at cursing someone out. I told him not to come to my house, call my number or dare talk to my mother again. If he did, I would tell the police, his parents, and his father's church what he had done. He was shocked at the way I was talking to him, but I think that he got the message and I did not hear from him again for years.

Years later, his mother called my mom and said that he wanted to see me. By this time, I had gotten married and had children of my own. There was no need to see or talk to him ever again. I told my mother then, just like I told her the day she made me talk to him, "I do not want to, nor will I ever need to speak to him again." I guess my mom still thought that he was the perfect man for me.

The rest of my high school years were a lot better. As I took hold of what happened to me with my boyfriend, I started to concentrate on what mattered. I needed to finish school with honors and get into a good college so I could get away from home. The relationship that I had with my mother was not the best in the world, so I learned to do what she asked so we could get along. I know people are going to think that I am crazy when I say stuff like that. I knew that my mother loved me, and I knew that my mom would do anything for me, but I also knew that my mom did not like me. Some people, including my oldest sister, say that my mother and I did not get along because we were so much alike. None of that mattered. What mattered is the fact that my mom and I had a love-hate relationship. I could see my mom and sister laughing and talking, but when I walk in the room, all the laughing stopped. Sometimes I would think that my mother did stuff just to see how mad I could get.

I was a straight A student. I worked a part-time job from the age of fourteen. I cooked, I cleaned the house, I worked in the garden (which seemed like year round). I went to and participated in church. I didn't get in trouble at school and I didn't hang out and party like most teenagers did. With doing everything that I could, I never could get my mother to like me. On my seventeenth birthday, my friends wanted to throw me a birthday party. Everything was planned for the party and my mom agreed to let them give me a party. My sister had to work and my mom was working on the second shift. My sister was not going to be able to come to the party and my mom wouldn't let me drive myself to the party. My mom insisted that they, she and my sister, would pick me up from the party. They both would be getting off work at eleven that night. My friends and one of my sister's friends offered to bring me home, but my mother would not have it. She would pick me up and that was final. The party was being held at a house about ten minutes from my mother's job so on the evening of the party, we were in the house partying hard. The music was blasting, the food was good, and a whole lot of people showed up for my party. I knew that I would have to leave when my mother came and I was cool with that. I didn't want to leave, but I was prepared to go. I kept looking at the clock and my watch. I was having one of the best days of my life. This was my party and it was just for me. Growing up, I had to share my parties with my first cousin because our birthdays were only three days apart. With my mother, not being able to afford to give me a party, I wasn't having the once a year birthday parties anymore as I got older. So tonight, I was having one of the best parties that I had ever been to. At exactly 11:15 that Saturday night, my mom burst into the house and yelled, "Laura, let's go." Laura was the nickname that my family called me. It wasn't my sister or someone else from outside coming to tell me that my mom was outside waiting for me. It was my mother and she was loud, she yelled again "Let's go." The entire room got quiet and everyone turned to look at me like oh my God. What in the world had I done to make my mother act like that? I don't know what made my mother act like that and at that moment, I didn't care. I left the party with my head down. I got in the car and looked at my sister with tears in my eyes. My sister had told me before my mother got back in the car that she tried to come in and get me, but my mother said she would do it. So, at that moment, I knew that my mother just wanted to embarrass me and she succeeded. We did talk on the way home and she said that I was supposed to be standing outside waiting for her, not inside partying. My thought was that if I was standing outside with all the boys when she got there, then she would have thought that I was fast. So, I was in the house partying and dancing, just having fun. I told her since I knew I had to leave, I wanted to party until it was time to go. That was the end of the conversation and I didn't speak to her again for months. I remember hearing her on the phone with one of her sisters saying she didn't know what was wrong with me. She told her sister that I had not spoken to her for months. If she asked me a question, I would answer with the shortest answer possible. If she came into the family room, I left and went to my bedroom or the living room. She did not have to tell me to do anything. I tried to anticipate what needed to be done and I would do it before she could ask. I would have dinner done or started before she got home from work. I would have her lunch packed for work and ready. I did my weekly cleaning chores without being asked or instructed to do before she could say anything. The laundry was done without being told to do it and if she wanted something extra done and asked me, I would get up and do it without any conversation. I still didn't understand why she was telling her sister that she didn't know what was wrong with me. My sister was in college now and she was living on campus. My brother was already out of the house with a home of his own, so it was just the two of us, living in misery.

By the time school started back for my senior year, I had so much on my plate that I really didn't have a chance to be angry. I became the co-editor of the school's yearbook committee and I was still a manager and scorekeeper for the school's basketball teams. I was a member of the pep squad, track team, and I was still taking dance lessons and performing whenever asked. After I had children, I think the reason I supported them so much in all their extracurricular activities is because my mother didn't support me in mine. Of all the things that I did, my mother saw me play ball once, she came to one track meet, and she came to my last dance performance in college. As I look back at things, my mom was not there when I was crowned 2nd runner-up Miss BHS, when I was on the homecoming court in the ninth grade, or when I was crowned 2nd runner-up Homecoming Queen in my senior year. No matter what I did, it was never good enough.

I know I sound bitter and I knew she loved me. I knew she was working to provide for us, so I never pushed the issue. When I became a parent, only death could keep me away from the events that my children were involved in. As my sister and I talk now about the relationships that we each had with our mother, we look back on the relationship that my mom had with her mother. It was a sorrowful relationship and I think because of the way that my mother was treated by her mother, she honestly didn't know how to show love. The effects of her marriage falling apart and the way that my grandmother treated her, there is no wonder that she had an issue with trust and love. I do not blame my mother, but as a child, I had a hard time understanding her. I also realized that I am so much like her, a hard worker and provider. I have a get it done mentality and I will figure it out no matter what attitude. The big difference is that I would not let anyone decide my future for me. I was not getting married because I was pregnant while she had a shotgun wedding. I worked where I wanted to or should I say, I worked where they hired me. She worked where her mother told her to. I made my own mind up and had to deal with the consequences of my choices. She did what she thought would make her momma happy, but still had to deal with the consequences of her mother's choices. My grandmother's opinions mattered to my mother and she tried her hardest to get her mother's approval. My mother's opinions mattered to me and although I listened, I made my own decisions.

In my soul, I knew I was a good person, even if I did not feel like my mom thought the same. I grew to become an independent, caring person. You can get me down, but you cannot keep me down. My mother never learned that her happiness did not depend on what other people said or thought about her. Her happiness depended on her love for herself. We can only control one person in life and that is thy own self. We cannot change people that do not want to be changed. We cannot make people do anything that they do not wish to do. No one walking on this earth has a Heaven or Hell to put us in, our strength comes from God. There is a song that we use to sing in the choir at church. "This Joy I Have," by Shirley Ceasar, tells us that the world didn't give it and the world can't take it away.

Secelia Tolbert

THIS JOY I HAVE THE WORLD DIDN'T GIVE TO ME.
THIS JOY I HAVE THE WORLD DIDN'T GIVE TO ME.
OH, THIS JOY I HAVE THE WORLD DIDN'T GIVE TO ME.
THE WORLD DIDN'T GIVE IT, AND
THE WORLD CAN'T TAKE IT AWAY.

SHIRLEY CEASAR

FORGIVING YOU MEANS,
I GIVE MYSELF PERMISSION
TO LIVE WITHOUT YOU
IN MY THOUGHTS.

SECELIA TOLBERT

GRANDMAMA

My grandmother was a bitter, unhappy woman and it showed in her children. If you think the relationship between my mother and I was shaky, the one between my grandmother and I was off the chain. If a family of women ever needed to seek out counseling, my family would benefit most from professional help. My grandmother's parents were killed when she was nine years old. As an only child, in early 1900s she was sent to live with relatives. Her father had money and land, but by the time she married my grandfather all her money and most of her land were taken from her. The family that she lived with said they had to use the money to raise her. As a child, herself and a black child at that, she had no outlet to seek help. When my grandfather told her that if she married him and bore his children, she would never have to work again in her life. She said yes and was married by the age of fourteen. She had her first child when she turned sixteen and true to his word, my grandmother never worked a commercial job in her life. She had seven children, so she worked every day, but at home. My grandfather expected breakfast, lunch, and dinner; a clean house, and his kids to be well taken care of. They raised all their food and did not depend on grocery shopping except for things such as sugar, flour, and cornmeal. They raised livestock, so all their meat was processed and stored for the year.

Living beside them, in the country, made for some exciting times. From working in the acres and acres of land for gardening, chasing the cows when they got out, to helping my mother and grandmother clean chitterlings on slaughter day, or running down from the top of the mountain with my sister. I remember once my sister and I got a whooping every day for about four days because we weren't hoeing the corn right. We were not putting enough dirt up around the stalks of the corn, so when Mama would come home she would check the corn and we would get another whooping. My sister and I thought that we were doing it correctly. We stayed outside in the hot sun hoeing that corn along with the other things that she had left for us to do, but it still was not right for her. On the fourth day, we had it right, but Mama said that we had to do it again the next day because you must stay on a schedule with the garden to have a productive crop. I can say now that if I had to, I would be able to survive off the land.

Back to my grandmother. We never really got along. I remember visiting my grandparents in the country when my parents were still married. My grandparents at that time did not have an inside bathroom, so we had to use the pot or go outside and use the outhouse. Neither one of those options worked for me. I remember my mom could squat outside without getting any pee on her. My sister learned to do it also, and of course, my brother did not have any problems, but little old me, I got wet every time I tried to squat outside. The pee would run down my leg, and my socks would get wet. I hated it. Going to the outhouse was out of the question, especially when granddaddy would say stuff like, "watch out for snakes." My grandmother would laugh at me because I couldn't go to the bathroom. I just really didn't understand why people didn't have bathrooms inside. When my mom told us that we were moving to the country next door to my grandparents, I cried until my mom assured me that we were going to have an indoor bathroom with running water. I remember one summer; my sister, brother, and I spent a week with my grandparents. During this time of life, some people only took baths on Saturday night so they would be clean for church on Sunday morning. The rest of the week they only washed off and hit the hot spots. The water was drawn from the well and heated on the stove. Because this was a rigorous procedure, you could only get two buckets of water. The problem with this is that everyone had to use that same water. Are you freaking kidding me?! We all had to share the same water to take a bath in and we had not had a bath in a week? Hell, to the highest no. I was like, I'm going first. I'm getting in that tub before anyone else if it kills me. Can you imagine getting in a tub of dirty water that is someone else's dirty water? My grandmother could not understand why we had a problem with that. We were too city. You damn right! Call it what you want to. City, uppity, I don't care.

The older I got, I realized that the issues that I had with my mom and grandmother, were the fact that they couldn't break me. No matter the situation, I would not bow or bend to them. I did not disrespect them or treat them badly, but I had my own opinion of things and of life, and I was old enough to think for myself. Yes, I still lived at home and depended on my mother for life, but some things just didn't make sense to me. When I was in my sophomore year of college, I became pregnant with my first child and what happened next people would not believe. My grandmother called me a slut and my mother tried to whip me with a belt because I would not have an abortion. You see, my pregnancy would be the first in the family that was born out of wedlock. If I didn't marry my boyfriend, I would have to have an abortion and I refused to do either. My mom actually chased me around the house yelling at me, because I refused to listen to her. The anger in my mom's voice and her eyes told me just how she felt about me.

My grandmother did not want anything to do with me. To her, I was the filth of the earth. Anyone having a child out of wedlock was the biggest sinner on earth. I was told I had to go in front of the church and ask for forgiveness. I wasn't doing that either. To have or not to have my child was my choice. No one was going to make me get rid of my baby. My grandfather, on the other hand, became my best friend. He would talk to me and let me know everything was going to be alright. No matter what anyone said or felt, he loved me and let me know he loved me.

The day I went into labor, my mom took me to the hospital and left me. I was in labor for thirty-three hours and she said she had to go to work. My grandmother didn't come at all and my sister was living out of the state at that time. My boyfriend finally showed up after she was born, but I had the most beautiful bald headed little baby girl. I finally had unconditional love. I was still living at home with my mother when I had my baby and the day that I could come home, I had to leave my little girl at the hospital because she had jaundice. I cried because I didn't want to leave her, but since I had already checked out at the hospital, they wouldn't let me stay. She remained in the hospital a couple more days and was released. My mother brought me home and she left me. My delivery was not the easiest. My daughter ended up ripping me when she came and I had to have fourteen stitches. Getting up and down to move around the house was not an easy task, but I had no choice but to get up and move. I guess my daughter staying at the hospital was God's way of giving me time to heal a little. There would have been no way for me to get up and down to get her with the pain that I was in. Those two days I was at home and she was still in the hospital was a life saver. When I could bring my baby home, my boyfriend came to take us to my mother's house. Of course, since we were not married, there was no way that my mother would let him stay and help me. So, I took care of my baby and myself.

The strange thing that happened after my little girl came home is that my grandmother and mother fussed over my baby as if this was a joyous occasion for the family. I sure do remember being threatened and almost beaten because I would not get rid of her. My mother and daughter had this incredible relationship, but my relationship with my mom and grandmother never really got any better.

I remember one Mother's Day, a few years after I had moved out, I went home to visit my mother and grandmother. My mother had to work that day, so I went to my grandparent's house to visit while I waited for my mother to get home from work. When I walked in, I said Happy Mother's Day Grandmamma, and her response was, "What did you bring me?" I told her I didn't have any money. I did not even have enough money to buy my mother a card. All I had was my love and she told me that wasn't enough. I laughed it off and said it's all I have. She just looked at me like I had something growing out of the side of my neck. She was in the process of cooking dinner and she asked me to finish frying the chicken while she got dressed so I starting frying chicken wings for her meal. I have had my second child, a son, by this time. My son asked if he could have a piece of chicken and I told him he had to ask Grandmamma. She said "no" the food was for her family that she had coming over for dinner. I stopped and looked and said, "What the fuck are we?" She looked at me like I had lost my mind. Mind you, she was cooking chicken drummettes. These are not the whole, pull apart kind, but the ones you buy from the Wing Factory. My son could not have a drummette, but I can stand here and fry it for you? I told my kids it was time to go and I looked at her and said don't let it burn. It was three years later before I stepped foot in her house. My family could not understand how I could stay away from her or the family. I did not stay away from the family, but I would go to family gatherings and meet family anywhere other than her house. My thought on the whole situation was that Daniel was put into the lion's den, he did not walk in there freely, so why I would put myself or my children somewhere that would harm them? I didn't lose anything in her house, especially love.

Three years later, I went to her house, because my aunts were giving my grandmother this huge birthday dinner and family from all over was coming into town for the celebration. I put on my big girl panties and went to her house to see her and the family. When I walked in the room, everyone stopped and stared like they had seen a ghost. My grandmother turned to see me and the first thing she said were, "Lawd child, how much weight have you gained?" Needless to say, I didn't go back until after she died.

My mother's relationship with her mother really never got any better. By the time of my grandmother's death, my mom still had not come to any terms of why her mother treated her the way she did. At my grandmother's funeral, we had to take my mother out of the service because she started screaming and asking her mother, "why didn't you love me," "what could I have done to make you love me, mamma." She was rocking and crying asking her mama to love her. That moment was a turning point in my life with my own mother. I did not want to wait until my mom was dead to have a better relationship with her. It took some time, but we did manage to work things out.

Secelia Tolbert

IF WE COULD LOOK INTO EACH OTHER'S HEARTS AND
UNDERSTAND THE UNIQUE CHALLENGES EACH OF US FACES, I
THINK WE COULD TREAT EACH OTHER MUCH MORE GENTLY,
WITH MORE LOVE, PATIENCE, TOLERANCE, AND CARE.

MARVIN J. ASHTON

A STRONG WOMAN

A STRONG WOMAN PERSEVERES WHEN HIT HARDEST COMING
BACK STRONGER THAN EVER. HER TROUBLES, PAIN, PAST HURT
AND WHOLE STORY, YOU WILL NEVER KNOW. BECAUSE SHE
STAYS DETERMINED, FOCUSED AND HAS A NEVER ENDING
GLOW!
A REAL MAN RECOGNIZES AND APPRECIATES HER STRENGTH!

UNKNOWN

Secelia Tolbert

LOVE OF MY LIFE

Once I started college, I realized the freedom of life. The joy of having control over my life. I felt this peace and calm of being around other people like me. I was working, I was dancing, and I was partying. Oh, I forgot studying and learning. I would leave home on Thursday and not come back until Sunday night. I partied with the Q's, the Kappa's, and the Alphas. I was asked to pledge a sorority, but because of financial reasons, I couldn't. I partied and partied. I loved to dance so I would be on the dance floor from the time I walked into a party. I met this great looking guy one night at a party and we danced the entire night together. A couple of days later, I went to my sister's dorm room and he was there because she was tutoring him in a science course. We were a couple from that day on. I feel in love and he was the person that was going to teach me what making love was all about. I had not been with anyone since that night long, long ago.

Everything that I did, I did with him in mind. I loved this man with every being of my soul. I woke up thinking about him and I went to sleep thinking about him. I was so in love, I really couldn't think of anything or anyone else. We dated for a year and then I found out that I was pregnant. I was so happy about the fact that I was having his child but neither one of us was ready to get married. He was a junior and I was a sophomore. His family was happy and mine was mad as Hell. Because I was pregnant, I could no longer dance, play basketball, or party like I used to. He continued to party and stay away all the time. This was the beginning of the end.

No matter what I asked or said, he had to go step with his brothers or go to another campus to visit other frat brothers. He was always going somewhere but when I asked if I could go or just expressed that I wanted to go, he said I didn't need to be there because I was pregnant. It did not matter to me that I was pregnant, I just wanted to be in the environment. I wanted to see people dancing and having fun. I wanted to be there. Being the fool I was, I just went along with it and what he said. I had other people, even some of his frat brothers coming to me and telling me I need to be careful. When someone that is supposed to be close to the other person says you need to be careful or watch your back, trust them and listen to them. However, no one or nothing would make me change my mind. I knew this man loved me and I was having his child.

My man was the most romantic man on this planet. He did things to make me feel as if I was the only woman on the earth. One day my mom called me at work to tell me I had a huge package that was delivered by the mailman and she wanted to open the box. I told her no and I would be there as soon as I got off work. When I got home, I saw this huge box and when I say huge, I mean HUGE. The box was almost as tall as I was and wider than me. It was packed in a box large enough that a stove or washer could fit in it. I opened it and there was a gigantic stuffed dog in the box, but that wasn't the best part. Tied in a bow on top of the dog's head was my engagement ring. As tears flowed down my cheeks, I looked up, and he was standing on the porch. He had driven from Atlanta to Bowdon (70 miles) on a motorcycle to surprise me. He said he had gone to my job to wait for me to leave and followed me home without me noticing him. He wanted to see my reaction when I got the ring. Things like this just made me fall in love with him all over again.

One time, I was having some problems with a man from work (I'll have to tell you that story later), my future husband drove to my job to follow me home and to make sure I was safe. By this time, he had left the school we were attending and started going to another school closer to his home. He could save more money this way since we had a child already. He was very smart and was getting a degree in Computer Engineering. He once took parts from different computers and made a desktop computer for me to have at home. However, programming computers was his specialty. With all my insecurities and all the things, I had floating around in my head, his being further away from me all of the time was creating a bigger problem.

At the time, I did not see or want to see all the red flags flying around in my face, hitting me upside the head, or stabbing me in my heart. Another woman, his ex-girlfriend, comes up to me and tells me that he was hers, always will be hers, and always had been hers. I should have believed her. I was so dumb because I'm having his child and I'm marrying him so he's mine. She shows up on more than one occasion and is persistent that he was hers. The fool that I was, he was no longer living close to me, but to her, so why wouldn't he be with her also. He stood there between the both of us and told me that he loved me and that she was just being messy and trying to cause trouble. He turned around and told her that he did not want her or want to be with her. I guess he told her. Three days before I gave birth to our daughter, she gave birth to their son, but I didn't find that out until seven years later.

August 18, 1984, I walked down the aisle on my father's arm as he was telling me, "you don't have to marry him." I think God was trying to tell me the same thing. My mom argued with the minister. My musician canceled on me a couple of days before the wedding. Thank you Genice Tiggs for coming through for me. I was using chairs from my uncle's funeral home (I had an outdoor wedding) but three people died the day before and they had to take the seats to the homes of the deceased. To top all of that, it stormed. When I say it stormed, I mean it stormed. The heavens were opening up with a vengeance. It rained so hard, I thought we were going to have to move the wedding inside of my little apartment. The worst thing that happened was that I decided that I wanted to put a Jerry Curl in my hair for the wedding. Take my advice and do not try something new with your hair a couple of days before your wedding. It wouldn't take because my hair was too soft and I had to cut all my hair off. Everything came out just fine. We got chairs from a church in Carrollton because my brother knew someone at the church. We used a DJ to play music and I had Endless Love sung by Genice. It finally stopped raining about an hour before the wedding. The wedding was beautiful and we had one of the best parties/receptions I had ever been to. My hair came out in a very low fro with tiny curls, my dad gave me away, and my mom continued to argue. I was now, Mrs. William Michael Tolbert, I. This was supposed to be the happiest day of my life, but it was one of the most stressful. I understand why brides are called Bridezillas.

Back to reality. My mom was upset because of the money I was spending on the wedding, but she didn't pay one red cent for anything. She told me that no one paid for hers, so she was not paying for mine. I thought this is what she wanted. Was she not the same lady that was trying to whip me with a belt two years earlier? The funny thing is, not one time did I ask her for her help. I worked and paid for the entire thing myself, except for my bridesmaid dresses. Thank you, ladies, for your help. As I look back at the pictures, I must tell you I'm sorry, they were some ugly dresses. Please forgive me. I even paid for the honeymoon. Wake up Secelia. What the hell is wrong with you?

My mom kept our daughter so we could go on our honeymoon, but she fussed about that as well. We had a weeklong trip to Fort Lauderdale, Florida and I must say, we had fun. We did some things that I promise you were not legal, but we didn't get caught. I'm sorry to the maids at the hotel because we had a blast in that room. We would swim in the hotel's pool, swim in the ocean, and we partied all night and slept all day. Well maybe not slept, but we stayed in the bed all day. We laughed and talked, we tried new things and did a whole lot of old things. The time together was good.

We were married for a good month and he still hadn't found a job. Did I not tell you that was one of the red flags flying high in my face? He was not working. That was one of the reasons that my mother was so upset. "If you didn't marry him when you got pregnant, what's the hurry now?" "Are you pregnant again?" "Is he helping you pay for anything?" I promise you, I heard it all, but I was in love and I couldn't see anything else other than I wanted to live with him. If I married him, he would be there with us. I would no longer have to worry about what he was doing so far away from me. I would see him every day. Let's be honest, I could control what was happening. My daughter needed her father in the house with her and it did not matter if he was working or not. I got this and I did not want to live in sin. (Hahahahaha) What a bunch of bull that was. What had I been doing all that time? By the fifth month of marriage, I would go to work, pay the bills and get home to find out that my husband wasn't there. He doesn't come home for hours at a time, but I'm still having to pay a babysitter. Sometimes he forgets to pick up our daughter and things started to get ugly really fast. I had been promoted to general manager at my job and began to make some pretty good money by this time, but my husband couldn't find a job in his "field." Remember I told you that he was smart. He wouldn't work at a fast food place or in a factory somewhere. He was too smart for that and if he was above that type of work, just another reason for my mother to be upset. We began to argue more than we talked. I would be upset because the house was filthy when I got home, the laundry was dirty, or nothing was cooked. And by this time, I found out that I was pregnant again, so I decided to get a divorce. Those damn red flags caught up with me and I couldn't take anymore.

Since I asked for the divorce and he wasn't working; my husband, the father of my children, the man that wouldn't get a job, the man that would not cook or do laundry, the man that I thought loved me unconditionally,

the man that said if I go through with the divorce, he would want
ALIMONY. What the hell, alimony, for what? The sad thing is because I
had married him when he didn't have a job and he was accustomed to living
by the means that I provided, I would by law pay him alimony. My attorney
suggested that I buy a house and get a new car. This would show the judge
that I couldn't afford to pay my lovely husband any extra money since I
would have to pay child care, there was no possible way for me to pay him
alimony. That worked, but damn now I had all these extra bills that had to
be paid.

The divorce was final so within six months of walking down the aisle,
I was getting divorced. The crazy thing is that I still loved that man. I missed
him, I missed the times we spent together, I missed being with his family, but
mostly I missed the loving. I needed someone to hold me at night someone
to whisper those sweet nothings in my ear. I remember times when we
would be yelling and screaming at each other, but we would get so excited
from all the arguing that we would make love for hours. I know it was
insane, but I wanted my husband back. He finally got a job, working with
his cousin. He started coming to spend the weekends with my daughter, and
I. He was there for the doctor visits and he was there when I gave birth to
our son. Or should I say, he tried to be there? He passed out during the
delivery and my mom came in to be my birthing coach.

I don't know if I was just a damn fool or I enjoyed being hurt, but I
remarried him. I thought I was the only fool to do this, but I have heard of a
lot of people marrying the same person more than once. After my son was
born, he really wanted to be a part of his children's lives. He had a son that
looked like him, a son that walked like him, a son that was full of joy and
would make you laugh just by looking at you. He was going to do anything
and everything to make his family work. Things were perfect for the first
couple of months. He moved back into my new house with his family. His
job was about two hours away from where we lived, so he needed to drive
the newer car to work so he wouldn't break down on the way to and from

work. He started getting home later and later. He said he was so tired, and traffic would be so bad that he would go to his mom's after work to relax and to let the traffic die down. Some nights he didn't get home until well past one in the morning. For him to get to work on time in the morning, he would have to leave by six which means he didn't get but a couple of hours of sleep every night. On the weekends, he would sleep or be gone all weekend, so I was still a married single mother.

He started dibbing and dabbing in drugs to the point that he was trying to grow some weed in my basement's crawl space. One day, my mother came to the house to drop something off. I was at work and my husband was keeping the kids. When my mom pulls up, my children were outside playing by themselves. The problem was that my daughter was only four and my son wasn't even walking yet. My son had crawled in the street and my daughter was trying to get him back in the yard. Normally, my mother would just yell and argue with me, but this time, she walked in the house and went off on my husband. When she got inside, she found his brother and my husband stone and the house smoked out from them smoking weed. She called me and told me she took the kids with her and Lord did I hear it from her when I picked them up. The argument I had with her was nothing like the argument that was had at home when I got there.

First, why were my children outside alone? Second, you knew my mother was coming, why on earth are you getting high with your brother that just got out of jail? Third, you knew what kind of relationship I have with my mom. Why? Why? Why? This fight was a fight of all fights. I don't think I ever have been this mad at any one human being before in my life. He put my children's life in danger, because of some weed. He denied everything that my mom was saying and told me she was lying, but the house smelled like weed and she had the children. What was I supposed to think?

Our second marriage was going downhill fast. He was staying out later and later and smoking more and more. One day I found a bag of white powdery stuff and asked what it was. He told me it was flour. Yeah, I'm a fool but not that big of an idiot. His job that he had with his cousin was in jeopardy because he was always late to work. His cousin suspended him and gave him a week off because of his tardiness. The company loved his work, but he was never on time and as a manager, his cousin needed him to do what the right thing because his cousin had put his own job on the line to hire him. The very first day back to work after the suspension, he was late and was fired that day. So here we go again, I'm married to a man that was not working. Only this time, he has started dealing with drugs. I really think, but I'm not sure, that he always dabbled with drugs, but after he got his job he had money to deal with the drugs more. He started to sell here and there to make money, but we all know that a drug dealer can't be a drug user. He once decided that he was going to cut the drugs to make some extra money, and he messed the drugs up. This was the beginning of the end of our marriage.

When people came to my door looking for him or money, it was time to say enough is enough. I pulled up to my house one day and a strange man walked from around the back of my house with a gun in his hand asking me where my husband was, I knew that was it. He had let his lifestyle put mine and my children's life in danger. I explained to the man that I had not seen him in over a week and I had no idea where he was. The guy left saying he would be back and to tell my husband he needed to get in touch with somebody with this crazy name. When he came home, he was terrified and looking around like someone was there or coming there. We started arguing about everything and nothing all at the same time. The arguing led to tussling and pushing until we were in a full-blown fight. This was something that I said that I would never do, fight in my own home. The fight escalated to the point to where I was running up the stairs to grab my gun, he was pulling me back down the stairs, and my earring ripped out of my ear. Blood was running down the side of my neck and I was furious. The look I saw in his eyes at that moment told me if I didn't get away I was going to die that night. He had that look like Satan himself had taken over his mind, soul, and body. I was fighting for my life and screaming all at the same time. He threw me on the sofa and was on top of me, but I wasn't giving in to him, I had to live. I had two children to take care of and Lord knows, I couldn't leave them to him to raise. You know how people say their life was flashing before their eyes? Mine wasn't. I was furious and I knew this man, my husband, had a black belt in karate and could kill me at any moment.

Suddenly, he got off me and ran towards my daughter. I jumped up and thought what the hell? Both kids were in the kitchen eating dinner when the fight broke out. My son was sitting in his high chair throwing food all over the place, but my baby girl had climbed up on a stool and called 911. He had to let me go to get the phone from her. She was on the phone with the operator and telling them that her mommy and daddy was fighting. This was just the time that I needed to get away. I ran upstairs to get the gun, but when I came back down the stairs, he was gone. My daughter said he left the house. I hugged her, for if it weren't for her, I probably would have not made it through the night. That was the last day that we spent together as husband and wife. He moved back home with his mom and continued his life without us. He told me that if I divorced him, he would spread all kind of dirt on me and smear my name to my family. One thing he said, he meant; if I divorced him, the children would be mine to raise.

That is what I did, raise my children. I might not have done everything by the book, but what book is that? I made some mistakes and did some things that were not morally right, but I am not perfect. At one point, my mother tried to take my children from me because I wasn't raising my kids to her standards. She even attempted to get my brother to sign a paper that stated I was an unfit mother. The Department of Family and Children Services found that I was doing no wrong. I was a single mother who was working, not on drugs, owned my own home, and my children were not in any harm. You see, once my husband and I separated, I started dating other men. She didn't like the fact that I had other men around my children, but they were no harm to my kids. Finding love from someone, anyone was my mission. I would work, I would take care of my babies, but I needed that someone that would just only love me back. At that time, one thing that I had not figured out yet was that I needed to love myself first. I had not found love with anyone else because I hadn't found love in me first. I needed to break the generational chain.

John C. Maxwell a well-known inspirational, motivational educator previously said, "Life is 10% of what happens to me and 90% of how I react to it." I could choose to continue as I was or I could decide to move on and make a new life. I know I was hard to live with and after I got sick, I realized how mean I really was. I would scream and yell for no reasons at all. I fired more people during a time of the month than any other time of the month. My daughter would take her brother and play with him when I was on my cycle just so I would not get upset. I honestly had no idea of the devil that was living in me, until after I had surgery. Maybe I drove my husband to use drugs just to handle my bipolar behavior. Oh, hell no, I will not take the blame for him being special. He still does not work even now and we have not been together since 1987.

The divorce procedures were simple. He had nothing and I did not want anything from him other than child support. The house was mine, I had a car, and he had a car. You take yours and I keep mine. The furniture was mine and the computer that he made was his. He had installed a commercial phone system throughout the house, that he wanted, but it became a part of the house and he could not have the system. He was ordered to pay me $188.00 per month for both of our children. $188.00 a month amounts to $2,256.00 per year to raise two children. Not $188.00 per child, but for both children. What was $188.00 supposed to do? It did not matter, I guess I should be used to doing things without his money anyways. I might as well not worry about it because he did not pay the child support.

Secelia Tolbert

I dropped the case after Mike signed his first contract with The San Diego Chargers. My babies' daddy owed me over $80,000.00 by this time. I knew that I would never see the money and the kids were grown. Maybe he could get his life together now, the hold on his license could be released, his taxes could be filed, or whatever he needed to live.

He would on occasions send me some money or call and tell me he left some money at his mother's house or one of his sisters had some money for me. I would have to drive to Atlanta to pick up the money. When I get there, it would be $30.00 or $50.00. For real, I drove all the way up here for this? Be grateful Secelia, he gave you something. At least, it could put gas in the car or pay for the kid's lunches at school. Oh wait, I just drove the gas out of the car, going to get this shit!!!

I would call Child Support Recovery trying to get them to help, but nothing ever happened. I remember one time CCR told me they could not find him to serve the warrant for neglect of paying his support. I had to give them addresses of where I thought he might be. I gave them every address I knew from his mother's, his sister's, his church, his girlfriend's, even his best friend's house. I gave every phone number that I had for anybody that might know where he was staying. I could call and get him, but they never could. I knew he was a trustee of his family church and that he sang in the choir. He had keys to open the church and was active in the church, so I gave all that information as well. It got to the point that if I knew where he was, I was supposed to call the sheriff's office and inform the sheriff department of his whereabouts so they would go and serve the papers. I called and told the sheriff that he would be at church on Sunday morning and two deputies went to give him the warrant. He was in the church when the sheriff's deputies walked in and nobody in the church would point him out. Even the pastor of the church said he was not there. Oh boy, did I stir up some trouble by doing this. I was called every name known to man for sending the sheriff to his church to embarrass him. How dare I do something that low down and dirty? He could not believe I would stoop so low just to get some money. He had already told me if I put him out and got a divorce, the kids were mine, and I had to raise them. He meant every one of those words.

Something happened and I really do not remember what it was, but he could not renew his driving licenses. He tried and CCR had put a hold on them for non-payment of child support. I did not know they had done anything. He called me and said he needed his license and wanted me to do something to fix this. Really asshole, you expect me to fix this for you? Nope, not me, not going to do a damn thing to help you. We were scheduled to go to court because my dear beloved ex-husband said he had been paying me child support the entire time we were not together.

The court procedures were actually funny. We ended up going to court three separate times to get me some help. The courthouse that we had to meet at was downtown Atlanta, which means I had to drive down to the court. I made my schedule so I was sure I would be able to get enough rest the night before and be off the entire day of court. I did not want anything to hinder me from being there. The judge that presided over our case was an older white man. When I say older, I mean, white headed and it looked like he had hair coming out of his nose and ears. He wore a hearing aid and thick glasses. As I sat in the courtroom listening to other cases before mine, I thought this judge is harsh. He spoke to people like they were crazy, he made Judge Judy look like a saint.

I did not have a lawyer because everything was already laid out in the divorce decree. There was nothing for me to worry about, however, now I was not so sure. I had no way of knowing if the judge would listen to anything that I had to say. TOLBERT VS. TOLBERT, please come forward. We both are standing behind two tables on the opposite side of the courtroom. "Mrs. Tolbert?" "Yes, sir." "You say that Mr. Tolbert here has not paid you any money on his child support?" "Yes, sir." "Now how could that be? I see here that there is an order in the divorce for him to pay you

$188.00 per month for two children?" He looks at me like what the f*** was I on. There is no way a man is in his courtroom for $188.00 per month for two kids. "Yes, sir that is correct." The Child Support Recovery documents showed all and any payments that had been made to me over the years. "Mr. Tolbert, I cannot believe you have not paid the child support order for your kids. There must be some mistake in the bookkeeping?" "Judge, I did not know I had to pay anything." I turned my head so fast I probably got whiplash. You did not know you had to pay child support? What the Hell? The judge starts to laugh and ask him, "Mr. Tolbert, how could you not know? It states it here explicitly in the divorce decree that you signed." "Sir, I did not know I was divorced. I didn't think the divorce was final." Now I am standing in the courtroom thinking you f'n mother***ker.

The divorce decree that the judge was reading was the one from Child Support and not the official order itself. The judge asked me if I had the original forms with the notary stamp, and I informed him that I did not have them with me, but I did have the papers at my house. So, the case was postponed for two weeks. I was to bring the original divorce papers. "We will see you in two weeks, Mr. Tolbert, I do not like people to play games with me." So, again I was going to have to wait. No money and no hope of getting any help.

Two weeks later, we stood before the same judge. Me with the original divorce papers and William with his Bible. Here we go again, "Mrs. Tolbert?" "Yes, sir." "Did you bring the divorce documents that I asked you to bring?" "Yes sir, I did." I hand the papers to the sheriff that was working in the courtroom. The judge flips through the pages and gets to the page where it says that William Michael Tolbert, I was to pay Secelia W. Tolbert the sum of $188.00 for the children April and Michael. The judge also looks at the last page where we both signed the final page of the divorce. The judge asked the sheriff to hand the papers to William so he could verify his signature. He instructed the sheriff to get some identification from William as the sheriff passed the document off. The sheriff took the ID and stood there while the signature was checked. "Yes, sir it is my signature. But I do not remember signing the paper." "That is not my problem sir, you signed it, therefore, you have to abide by the decision." The judge hands the ID back without even looking at the thing. I figured he's probably used to people saying that's not my signature and once he gets some ID, the lie changes, so he got the ID first relieving us all from that lie. Now, what? What will come out of his mouth this time? "Sir, I have paid Mrs. Tolbert child support." Man, please with this shit. The judge looks at him like he could chew him up and spit him out. "Mr. Tolbert, are you saying that you have paid child support to your wife?" "Yes, sir I have." "Mr. Tolbert, we have no record of you paying. Do you have any receipts for payment?" "No, sir. I did not give her cash. I bought things for my children or I would give the children the money when I would see them." "Mr. Tolbert, can you prove that you have given the children money or do you have receipts for purchases for the children?" "Yes, sir I do." "Where are your receipts, Mr. Tolbert?" "I did not bring them, sir." "Mr. Tolbert, what did you think you were coming to court for today?" "Sir, I don't understand?" "Why did you think that you were coming to court for today?" "Child support." "But you didn't bring any receipts?" "No, sir." The case was postponed for two more weeks.

The previous two times I did not bring the kids with me, but this time, I felt that I needed too. If he was saying that he gave the kids the money, I needed them to say they got the money or they didn't. I was sitting in the court with the kids when he and his mother walked in. He had this huge yellow envelope stuffed full of stuff and his Bible. He was shocked to see the kids with me. "Why did you bring them with you?" "They wanted to come." I lied. I could tell he was furious. He sits down on the opposite side of the courtroom, but his mother sat down with the kids. She proceeds to ask them why they had not called her or came to see her. My thought was, how were they supposed to get there and why haven't you called them? I kept my mouth shut as this was not the time or the place. My mother-in-law and I had never had a problem with each other and I loved all my in-laws. However, she starts to tell me that us having to come to court did not make any sense. She never took anyone of her children's fathers to court for child support. She never made a man pay for her children, they would give them whatever they wanted. Now I understand my problem.

We were called up to the front and the circus started again. "Mr. Tolbert, I need to see your proof or I need to see some money." "Excuse me, sir?" "I need to see your proof of payment or I need to see some cash." "Sir, I don't have any evidence." The judge looked at him with these piercing eyes and looked like he could strangle him with his own hands. "What do you mean, you do not have any proof? What is that you have in the envelope?" "Just some paperwork I was going to work on while I was waiting." The judge looks at the Bible. "Mr. Tolbert, is that your Bible?" "Yes, sir." "You know that is just a book of words unless you are living by them. One thousand dollars to purge." "I'm sorry, I don't understand?" "One thousand dollars to purge," the judge says again, but William still didn't understand what the judge was saying. Hell, I did not understand either. The deputy sheriff says, "One thousand dollars to get out of jail." William skin tone went pale. The judge had taken out his hearing aid and started cleaning it, like he was saying I don't give a damn about what you are saying, take your ass to jail.

Finally, the judge puts his hearing aid back in and starts to talk to William. "Mr. Tolbert, are those your children sitting in the back of the courtroom?" "Yes." "Mr. Tolbert, records show the last time you gave some money it was a couple of years ago and it was only $30.00. Do you understand that your children need to eat? When you eat, you need to think that your kids need to eat. When you lay your head down to sleep, you need to think that your children need to have a place to lay their heads down. When you get dressed, you need to think that your kids need clothes. Is that your son, I know his shoes cost a lot? I can see that he eats a lot. How do you expect Mrs. Tolbert to support them?" "She has a job and makes good money." This time, it was the judge that changed colors. "One thousand dollars to purge. Get him out of here." He was handcuffed and escorted out of the courtroom.

I was informed by CCR that once the money was paid, he would be released. He now had to pay the $188.00 plus $50.00 to start to catch up the arrears. A total of $238.00. This money would be a big help in taking care of the kids, but I never got another penny from him. His mother and stepfather paid the money to get him out of jail. He never paid again. Of course, my mom could not understand why I did not pursue him being locked up. What good would that do? He was not going to get a steady job, he was not going to send the children any money. All I would be doing would be for nothing. I decided to focus on taking care of my kids and living a happy life. He would have to meet his maker one day and oh how I would love to be a fly on a cloud that day. I asked one day, what was he going to do when he knocks on the Pearly Gates? "Whatcha mean?" He tried to play it off like he didn't know what I was talking about. Baby, one day you are going to die, and you know God does not like people to mistreat his children. "I have not harmed my children." That's a matter of opinion. Not feeding them, giving them shelter, nourishing them, and giving them love is mistreating them. You know it is not about the money, it is about spending time with them. Showing them that you love them and miss them. You can't even pick up the phone and call them. The conversation was over, he did not want to hear that. It was my fault he was not with his kids, I should have never put him out. I had to throw one more thing at him. "One day you will need them, who is going to wipe your ass when you get old?" "Which one of your children do you expect to take care of you or come see you when you go to a nursing home?" "Who do you think will bury you?" "Who will cry at your funeral?" He hung up.

I've had some ups and down with my children, but I know that they know how much I love them. They know that if anything and I mean anything ever happens to them, I will be there. I do not care how far I have to drive or fly, I will figure out a way to get to my babies. The mama bear in me comes out and I will **** (place any four-letter word you want) about my babies.

Mike signed a contract with The San Diego Chargers in March of 2008 and I received a letter from Child Support Recovery around the same time. The letter stated because of inactivity the case was going to be closed. I could call the agency to let them know I wanted to continue with the process and I wanted them to continue to search for him. Both of my children had gone to college and graduated so I did not need the hassle of dealing with William anymore. I chose to close the case and let over $80,000.00 go. I was informed that if I continued the process, that there still would be a hold on his license and his income taxes. I talked to both kids and Mike said, "We don't need it anymore, mama. Let it go." Now, April, my accountant said, "Don't drop the case, if you don't want the money, I do." That's my child!

My mom, on the other hand, was adamant that I should not drop the case. You deserve the money, it is yours. You had to do what he was supposed to do, so he is just paying you back what he owes you. I dropped the case. I would never see that money and even if by some chance he finds the same God that I serve and he decides that he wants to say, "Hear you go, this is for you." I doubt that, so I know I will never see the money anyway.

I have people asking me all the time if my ex, the children's father, has reached out to Mike. It is hard to explain, but NO! I say it was difficult to explain because I only remember him coming to a recreation football game when Mike was on the Homecoming Court. I remember him coming to one baseball game and a basketball game once Mike got into high school. He has never seen April perform or play in anything. When Mike was in college at Coastal Carolina University, which is only a five-hour drive from Atlanta, he called Mike and asked for some tickets. Mike told him that I got all his tickets, and if he needed a ticket, he had to call me to get them. I never got that call. After Mike, had made it to the league, William called me and asked me for Mike's phone number. I told him that I would have to ask Mike if it was okay to give the number to his father. He did not understand why I had to get permission to give out the number. "I'm his father, you don't have to have permission to give me his number." My response to that statement was, "most fathers already have their children's number." "Well when you speak to him, tell him I would like to talk to him." I laughed and said, "I talk to my child every day." Mike agreed because he said he wanted to talk to him and see what he needed to say. I was hesitant because not one time did he ask for April's number. If he was concerned and wanted to repair their relationship, he had more than one child. Other people were telling me to give him a chance. Why now, why after his son signed a contract to play in the NFL? It was three days later before he called back to get the number. I gave it to him, and that was that.

He finally called Mike in San Diego, California and told him that he was proud of him. Mike said the conversation between the two of them went something like this; "I'm proud of you son, you graduated from college, and now you are living your dream." Mike was pleased with the way the conversation was going, and they continued to talk. I guess the conversation should have ended then because it went way south after that. "If you ever need anything, just call me." "WHAT, IF I EVER NEED ANYTHING. IF I EVER NEED ANYTHING. NIGGER, I DON'T NEED YOU. I NEEDED YOU WHEN MAMA WAS WORKING TWO AND THREE JOBS TO TAKE CARE OF US. I NEEDED YOU WHEN WE DIDN'T HAVE ANY MONEY AND WE HAD TO EAT RAMEN NOODLES EVERYDAY FOR A MONTH BECAUSE WE DIDN'T HAVE ANY GROCERIES. HELL, I STILL NEED MY TRICYCLE YOU PROMISED ME WHEN I WAS TWO. NIGGER, I DON'T NEED YOU!!!!! MOTHERFUCKER, I'M A FUCKING MILLIONAIRE NOW, WHY WOULD I NEED YOU?"

We didn't hear from him again until the death of my mother. His sister called and said that he wanted to call and speak to me, so I let her give him my new phone number. He did call and the conversation was polite and short. This would have not been the time to piss me off. He came to my mom's services and as Mike and my nephew was helping me back to the car, he stopped me to say hi. Mike pulled me on and told me we must go. As I was getting in the car, Mike bent down and asked me how in the hell did I marry that nigger. I explained to Mike that the man that he saw standing on the porch of the church was not the man that I fell in love with. That man has let drugs and time control him. I informed Mike that the man that I loved and married was an athlete who was built, handsome, and smart just like he was for they look just alike.

The last time I spoke with William was three years ago, after Mike signed with the Carolina Panthers. He called and said that he lived in Charlotte and wanted to go to a game. I informed him that he was more than welcome to go to any game that he liked. I have never stopped him from seeing his son play. He wanted to go to a game with ME! Nope, not happening. Not today or any other day. Can't see, won't do it. What the HELL?????? He wanted me to get tickets for him to go to a game and he wanted me to pick him up and let him sit with the family and me. Now he knows me better than that. He assumed I got free tickets. Mike gets two tickets to the game, and unless his wife is going to let you have her seat, I feel for ya, brother. Ticket master sells tickets 24/7, you can buy as many tickets as you would like. "Why can't you get me a ticket?" "How can you ask your son to get you a ticket and you couldn't even buy him a happy meal?" Conversation ends. Have not heard from him since.

Mike called me this past Thanksgiving and said he needed to talk to me about something. The type of relationship that Mike and I have, if he tells me he needs to talk about something, it is serious. He wanted to know how I would feel if he reached out to his father. He was thinking that he did not want something to happen to his father and he never had let his father know how he felt about him not being in his life. I told him, he is a grown man and if that is what he wanted to do it would be okay with me. I could forgive my father and accept my father after he was not there for me as I was growing up and it would be his decision to do the same with his father. What happened to his father and I was just that, between his father and me. Mike, is a father himself now and can see life with different eyes. I told Mike how proud I was of him and the father, husband, brother, and son that he has turned out to be. He bathes the kids, he feeds them, he cleans the house, he cooks, but he loves his family. The love that he has for his family is so true, and it is precious to watch him with them. When I told Mike that I was proud, he said he learned from the best. Now you know my head swole up, and I was like, he thinks I was the best. He said no, I learned from my father. My eyes popped out of my head. What the hell is he talking about? He said he learned what not to do. He never wanted his family to want for anything or wished he was around. He never wanted his kids to feel the way he felt growing up. Well damn!

Secelia Tolbert

**WHEN THINGS ARE NOT ADDING
UP IN YOUR LIFE,
START
SUBTRACTING THINGS**

Bishop Dale C. Bronner

TAKE YOUR PAST

AND
TURN IT INTO
THE
FUEL THAT
MOTIVATES
YOUR
FUTURE.

UNKNOWN

Secelia Tolbert

MISERABLE PEOPLE

FOCUS ON WHAT THEY HATE ABOUT THEIR LIFE.

HAPPY PEOPLE

FOCUS ON WHAT THEY LOVE ABOUT THEIR LIFE.

SONYA PARKER

STALKER II

Out of everything that I could and would think of as a single parent, I never in my wildest dreams thought that I would be stalked by a person. What did I have for them? What could I do to upset someone to the point that they wanted to harm me? Well, I found out the summer of 1986. It started in 1985 at the restaurant where I was working. There was this young man that had mental issues and he would hear voices or see people, but if he was taking his medication, he would be okay. He worked for our restaurant a couple of times and each time he left, it was because of having a breakdown. His father would send him for treatment and after he had come back home, we hired him back. Let's call him Patrick to keep him safe now. Remember, he was one of the best people I knew, and I loved working with him if he was on his meds.

Patrick was an opener for us and he came in with myself and one other person to get the restaurant opened on time. On one occasion, while we were preparing produce cutting lettuce, tomatoes, and onions, he was supposed to be getting the hamburger meat ready to cook once we opened. Suddenly, meat started flying across the room. A blob of meat heat Terri on the side of her head. Beef flew across the room and landed in the sink of lettuce. Terri and I ran to the office and locked the door, called the store manager and Patrick's daddy. His father came to get him, and he was gone away for a couple of weeks. We all knew he had some problems and we had to be careful with him. He came back to work and was doing the same great job he always did (if he had his meds).

Until, the next occasion. Again, Terri and I were preparing to open the restaurant and Patrick started screaming. He was in the back room with a broom and he was screaming that the birds were at him. He was swinging the broom and hitting products off the shelves. He was yelling, "they're trying to get me." Again, we ran and called his father, again he was gone for a couple of weeks, and again we hired him back.

The final problem that said we no longer could let him work at the restaurant happened a couple of months after he came back to work. We could tell the new medicine that he was on was stronger than before and he wasn't his usual happy self. He seemed to be depressed and standoffish when he was at work. He was still a hard worker and one of the best grill operators that we had, but he was slower than normal, and he had to have the orders repeated over and over again, which is something that we never had to do before. On this one day, his last day with us, Patrick went into the walk-in cooler, but he stayed longer than it should have taken anyone to get any product. We were asking where he was, maybe he came out and went to the restroom. He had not gone to the restroom and when he walked out we were all in shock. Patrick had taken a serrated knife into the cooler with him and proceeded to shave his head with the knife. He was bleeding from cuts on his scalp. Patches of his scalp were laying on the cooler floor and he still had the knife in his hand. The general manager called 911, and we had to close the restaurant down for a couple of hours. The crew was in total shock and Patrick was on his way to the hospital. His father arrived and rode with him to the hospital in the ambulance. No one at the restaurant was harmed, but it was too scary with the knife. The safety of the other employees and customers became a real issue now, so the decision was made that he would not be able to return after this incident.

He returned home and came to get his job back, but I had to tell him he could no longer come back. By the time, he came back after this, I had become the General Manager, and I was the one that had to deal with him. He was so upset, but he left, and I didn't hear from him again until he showed up at the drive through with his father one day, mad as hell. He asked for me, and when I went to the window, he starts screaming at me about trying to stop him from getting a job, and he was going to get me. I was like what in the hell are you talking about, but he tells me that I gave him a bad reference, and he knew about it.

The only person that I had given a reference to about him was to a former manager that previously worked for our company, but now the manager was working at a pizza joint. This manager also worked for us way before Patrick was ever employed by the restaurant, so he had no idea of the things that we had been through with Patrick. I knew that I should not have said too much because of the privacy laws. What can be said when giving references about former employees changed because of me. I had told the manager about everything that Patrick had done, and he should not hire him. I told him about all the things that we had encountered with Patrick and that it would be very dangerous to hire him at his restaurant. Well, needless to say he hired Patrick anyway and then proceeds to tell him everything that I said. If you are going to hire him, why tell him what I said?

Patrick was so mad, he said he was going to get me. Get me, what you talkin' about Willis? I spoke with the police, and they said there was nothing that they could do because he had not done anything to me personally. Mind you, this is 1986 and the laws were different then. Patrick started coming to the restaurant, but he wouldn't order anything. He would come and sit in the dining room. He would drive through the drive-thru and ask for a cup of water. He would come when I wasn't there and tell the employees to leave a message for me. He would show up at closing time and just sit outside of the restaurant. After calling the police repeatedly, the police decided that I had an actual problem, and they would look into it. The police did go and speak to him, and his father and they told the cops that they were just messing with me and didn't mean to do me any harm. He promised the police that he would stop. The police came back to me and told me that I had nothing to worry about they had spoken to him, and he had promised to quit bothering me.

The very next night when I worked, I had to take the closing deposit to the bank and thank God, we always had a police escort to the bank, but Patrick was sitting on top of his car at the bank as we drove up to the bank. The officer that was with me had no idea of the problems I had with Patrick and just drove off after I dropped the money. Now I had an issue, where do I go? The restaurant is closed, I don't want to drive home with him following me, and I did not want to go pick up my kids from the babysitter, but she was waiting for me. This was before we had cell phones so I couldn't call anyone from my car. I went ahead and drove to the police station and told them what had happened and they followed me to pick up my kids and said they would get in touch with the officer that had my case in the morning. I was so paranoid that it was hard for me to sleep or function.

I had a permit to carry, but I couldn't take the gun inside the restaurant with me, which means that if anything happened in the restaurant, I was not protected. If I was getting off and he was outside, with my gun in the car, I had to get to my car before I could protect myself. It was just the most stressful situation any one person should go through. My brother would come by and check on me on his off days, I got my mom's shotgun to keep in the house, and I had my gun in my hand when leaving or going inside my house. I started having my mother pick up my kids and taking them home with her if I had to work the closing shifts. This way I didn't have to worry about them and if they would be in harm's way. The sheriff's department started following me home and checking out my house after I made the night deposit. The detective that had talked with Patrick earlier said they couldn't find him and his parents had no idea where he was. He had stopped working and had stopped coming home, which also means he was not taking his medication.

Patrick drove through the drive-thru one Thursday afternoon and told the cashier to give me a message. "Tonight, is the night." That was the only thing he said, and the cashier told the manager on duty, and they called me as soon as they got the message. I was terrified, scared wasn't even the word to use. The owner of the restaurant said I could stay at home, and they would cover my shift, but I didn't want to be at home alone. So, I went to work as I normally would. The police were informed of the message, and they made regular welfare checks on the restaurant and me. At closing, in between, the police visits, one of the employees saw Patrick outside. We were defiantly going crazy in the restaurant, what was he going to do? Was he messing with my car? Why hadn't the police seen him? Why in the hell did I come to work? Did I put the other employees in danger, by being there? I called the police back, but by the time they came back, he was gone again. So, on this particular night, when the police pull up to escort me to the bank, there were two different officers in two separate cars. One officer gets out of the car and comes into the store and walks me to my car. He checks the car out and makes sure nothing is wrong with my vehicle. They both escort me to the bank, one drives ahead and gets to the bank first, the other drives directly behind me. Once I got to the bank, both officers get out of their cars guns were drawn ready for action. Nothing happens, but the night wasn't over yet.

Like the previous nights, the officers escorted me home and this night both officers get out. One officer goes inside to check out the inside of the house while the other officer checks outside around the house. Again, nothing is out of place, and nothing is wrong. They tell me they could not stay, but an officer would always be around the corner and patrolling in my area, in case I needed them. Okay, I can do this, but would I be able to sleep tonight? My brother was at work, but his boss knew what was going on, and he told me he would take off and come stay with me, but I couldn't let this one man control my life. So, I told my brother to stay by the phone and come if I called. He tells me to push the TV in front of the door and leave all the lights on in the house. Nobody would bother me or would think twice before they did if they saw all the lights on. I did exactly as he told me, I pushed the big floor model TV in front of the front door. I moved a shelf in the kitchen in front of the back door, it wasn't that heavy but if pushed a whole lot of stuff would fall off. I turned the radio on and left every light in the house on. I went to my bedroom, moved the dresser in front of the door, and had the TV on in there as well. I laid down on the bed, too scared to go to sleep. I had the shotgun lying across my lap and the pistol lying on the nightstand right next to the phone. By this time, it's almost three o'clock in the morning, and I'm exhausted. I fall asleep lying on the bed. I woke up when I heard a noise and my house was totally black dark. No lights, no TV, no radio, nothing.

I grab the shotgun, and I slide down on the floor. With my back, up against the wall, I was sitting in the corner with the gun pointed towards the door. I was panicking and didn't know what to do. I called 911 because they are supposed to be right around the corner. The operator asked me if the power was out at the other houses in the neighborhood. How was I expected to know? I wasn't going to look out the window, what if he was standing outside? The operator told me, it could just be a coincidence and the power was out. They couldn't send a police officer every time I got scared. I wanted to curse her out, but I needed them. I stood up and took a quick peek out of the window, and all the other duplexes had power on. What wait, how did they have power and I didn't? Now I'm terrified even more. She was talking about stay calm, and the officer was on the way. I had called my brother also, and he was on his way. I stayed squatted down in the corner talking to Patrick like he was in my house. I told him if he was going to do something come on and let's do it. I said that I had both guns, and I knew how to use them, so let's do this. I was talking to myself, he said nothing back. That made it even worse because I had no idea where he was. If he answered me, I would, at least, know where he was located inside of my house. It seemed that it took forever for the police and my brother to come to my rescue. I was crying now and really tripping in my head. I heard a car pull up and then I heard my brother screaming my name. He wanted me to move the stuff from in front of the doors, but what if Patrick was in the house with me. I told my brother to stay outside until the police got there and he could come in with them. I didn't want Patrick to be outside with my brother and hurt him trying to get to me. The police arrived in full force. There were police cars everywhere. They were talking to me from outside trying to tell me to come to the doors. I still didn't know if Patrick was inside of my house. They said he couldn't be because the stuff was still in front of the doors. But what if he came in and moved it back? I had to take that chance and get to the help that came to help me.

I reminded the police that I had both guns and that I had them on me. They laughed at me and told me they were coming around to the back door and coming in. They could move that shelf easier than the TV. I didn't care if everything broke, but I was too terrified to move. They came in and checked out the house and they didn't find Patrick anywhere. I come out of my room, and they checked it out. Patrick is not in my house. The problem is that I have no power and the duplex connected to me did not have power. The rest of the community had power, now how in the hell did that happen? Patrick (or someone) had shot out the transformer box that went to my duplex. The officers said you could see the bullet hole in the box and smoke coming from the transformer. The transformer blowing is probably what woke me up, and if I hadn't woken up, he probably would have done something to me or to the duplex like burn it down. The thought of that was crazy, I had moved everything in front of the doors to keep him out, but I was also keeping me in. If the house was on fire, how would I have gotten out?

There was enough now for the police to go after Patrick and press charges. The power company could press charges. But again, where was he? No one had any idea of how to find him. Where was, he staying and who was helping him hide? His father was questioned again, and they found him the next day. He admitted to doing everything and said he was not going to hurt me he just wanted to scare me. Charges were still pressed, but he has a mental problem so he didn't get jail time. He did have to go back to the hospital and stay for some years. By the time, he was supposed to get out of the hospital, I had moved to another city, and hopefully, he had forgotten all about me. I had put all of this behind me, and I had not seen or thought about him in over ten years, until one day I went to visit my mother and I was sitting at a red light and directly across from me on the opposite side of the light, Patrick sat in a red car. He stared at me as I was driving by and I stared at him as I drove by. I continued looking in my rear-view mirror hoping he didn't turn around. I hit the expressway and got the hell out of there. The police had warned me that he would be getting out, but it didn't bother me until I saw him. He didn't follow me, to my knowledge and I have not seen or heard from him. I pray that God has healed him, and he went on with his life.

I can promise you that I never gave another reference to another manager that was not positive. I don't care if it was Jesus Christ himself calling me asking, "Did so and so work for you?" Yes. "Would you rehire them?" Yes or No but nothing else. "Can you tell me why they left your employment?" No. "Are they trustworthy?" I'm sorry, they worked from Date? To Date? And they can be rehired or no they cannot be rehired. Have a great day. If you don't learn from your own mistakes, you are a fool.

ALWAYS KNOW WHERE YOU'RE GOING,
BUT NEVER FORGET WHERE YOU
CAME FROM.

SECELIA TOLBERT

IN MY SHOES, IT GETS TOUGH SOMETIMES...YES.

IN MY SHOES, IT IS UNFAIR SOMETIMES...BUT.

I WOULDN'T TRADE ANYTHING FOR MY JOURNEY; I LOVE BEING....

A WOMAN CHOSEN BY GOD!

UNKNOWN

CANCER CAME KNOCKING

The word CANCER had been that word that everyone in my family feared. You see in 1984, my mamma's baby sister, Helen, died of breast cancer. She was the aunt that everyone loved, the one that we all called our favorite aunt. I could talk to her about anything and everything. She was the free spirit of the family, always laughing and having fun. She worked as an interior decorator and real estate agent. She was the best-dressed person that I knew. She just simply loved life. I could never figure out why she was so full of love, and the rest of the family had so much anger. She loved my baby girl, April and it is still uncanny how much my daughter looks like my aunt still today. Aunt Helen was my refuge in times of need. I could call her, and we would talk for hours. I could just drop by her house or office and see her anytime I wanted. My daughter loved herself some Aunt Helen. By the age of two years old, my daughter could not pronounce Helen's name correctly, so it sounded more like Hel-leeeen, but it was so cute the way she said it. Aunt Helen loved it and would just light up when I brought my baby to see her.

Christmas of 1983, my daughter, my mother, and I had Christmas dinner with Aunt Helen. As an interior decorator, Aunt Helen would decorate her house so unusual during the holidays. This year under her tree, she had placed the white shipping peanuts around the tree as it was snow. The tree had only silver and purple ornaments on it with string lights. It was so beautiful, but the most beautiful thing was my baby was sitting under the tree tossing the peanuts in the air and laughing. She played for hours under the tree. The day was so special, and then Aunt Helen told us that she had found a lump in her left breast, and she had made an appointment for a couple of weeks to have it checked out. We prayed, and we just knew everything would be alright, but she told us she felt this would be her last Christmas with us. There were questions about when she had found the lump and why hadn't she already gone to the doctor. She said she had found the lump a couple of months earlier, and since she worked for herself, she didn't have insurance, so she was waiting to go to the doctor. She also didn't want to know her diagnoses and spoil the holiday season for us all.

In January, Aunt Helen went to the doctor and the news was not good. She had stage four breast cancer, and the type of cancer she had was a very fast-spreading type. The doctors didn't think she would make it but maybe another six months. Our world was rocked. How to deal with this? She had her left breast removed, and a very intensive treatment plan was started. We had never had to deal with anything like this before. I can tell you, that Aunt Helen was the strongest person that I have ever met or seen on this earth. She worked right through her treatment. She was still sold houses from her hospital beds. When she felt good, she would go out and work on her decorating projects. She would have setbacks and have to go to the hospital for brief stays. My mother and Aunt Helen flew over the country looking for different doctors and different cures. However, the results were always the same; she was dying, and there was nothing we could do about it. Every time I would visit her, I would take my daughter, and she had to bring Aunt Hel-leeeen a gift, whether it was a flower, a stuffed animal, or some Bankhead Fish (Aunt Helen loved Bankhead Fish Market). The smile on Aunt Helen's face when we came in the room was priceless.

The cancer was evading the left side of my aunt's body. It was like night and day. Her left side was rotting away while the right side seemed perfectly normal. I watched as my mom would change her bandages and green puss oozed from the hole left from where her breast use to be. When the bandages were off, it smelled so bad, and she would just cry from the pain. She was in so much pain, but she never let it get her down. I watched as the swelling was so severe on the left side of her body that her skin was popping away from her nail bed. The left side of her body was dying. All of her hair had come out, but on the days, that she could, she would put her wig on and still go to work. I remember the last couple of weeks that she was alive, she was too weak to leave the house, but she made this high dollar sale of a commercial building right from her bed. With no insurance, she was still trying to make sure her debts were taken care of. The last time I saw her alive, was the weekend before she passed. We talked, and she told me that she loved me and that my daughter was in her will. I knew she loved my baby, but out of all her nieces and nephews, and her only child, she had left something to my baby. We just sat together with each other, until I had to go.

My uncle called me to tell me that she had passed, and I just sat down on the floor and cried. Even knowing that this day was coming, it still was the hardest thing I had ever had to deal with. I drove to Atlanta to be with my family and to be there for my mamma. Her baby sister was gone. We could rejoice in the fact that Aunt Helen was not in any more pain. She had suffered enough, and her body just couldn't hold on any longer. Aunt Helen had already planned her funeral, there was nothing for us to do, but show up. She did not want that tear-jerking, sad funeral. She wanted everyone to be happy and rejoicing in knowing that she was all right and in a better place with The Lord. Her pastor preached to us and told us if we wanted to see her again, we had to start living right. The death of my aunt was the hardest on my granddaddy; he had to get up and walk out of the service. How was he supposed to bury his baby girl? THIS CANCER THING SUCKS!!!!!!!

Years later, cancer was back. My oldest sister told us that she had to have exploratory surgery. When the doctor came to speak with the family, it was not the news that we wanted or expected. She had some of her lymph nodes removed along with the tumor. We were going to go through this again, but this time, it was my sister. Her treatment started with chemotherapy and followed up with radiation.

My brother-in-law was a trooper. While waiting at the hospital, we sat and talked about Karla and life in general. I have always known that he loved my sister, but that day I realized just how much. He was scared and nervous the entire time, but he stayed encouraged in the fact that she was a praying woman, and God had her. When the surgery took longer than planned, we both were a little worried, but we knew that God was in control.

She came home after a brief stay in the hospital to recover. Her chemotherapy started briefly after returning home. My brother-in-law made sure that she had whatever she needed. He wanted to cook dinner for her one Sunday, but he didn't know how to cook collard greens. He asked me to show him, he stood at the sink with me and helped me cut and wash the collards as my sister rested. After all the men in my life have cheated on my mother, my grandmother, and myself, it was refreshing to see a man that loves and cherishes his wife. A man that did whatever it took to make sure his wife was comfortable.

She continued to work as a chemist, but the chemo would make her sick. She decided to have her treatment on Fridays that way she would feel better by Monday for work. Her hair started to come out by the hand fulls. All of her life she has had that long thick, shiny hair that hung down her back. And other than a trim, she had not cut her hair. Once it started coming out, she was so upset. She cried saying, "my hair." There was nothing that anyone of us could do to comfort her about losing her hair.

She would wear scarfs of different colors to hide the fact that her hair was gone. Sometimes, I can be a little niave, I sat in her family room talking to her trying to understand what was going on with her body. She was saying that as she showered, her hair was just falling in the bottom of the shower. I asked, all of it, and she told me yes. I looked at her with a confused state of mind and waved my hand over my body from the top of my head down and asked, "All." "Yes, ALL!!!!" Never had I thought about a cancer patient losing all of their hair. But it makes sense if the hair on your head falls out why not everywhere else.

Every Christmas our family and my brother-in-law's family comes to their house to celebrate the holiday. This particular year, for my sister's Christmas gift, I went a did something without telling anyone. She came to the door when I rung the doorbell, she looked at me and cried. I shaved the hair on my head. I told her it was just hair, and it would grow back. We could let our hair grow back together. I wasn't sick, but I could try and make her feel better. The chemotherapy was working, and her next step in treatment was going through radiation.

She has been cancer-free for eight years, and we pray to God that she continues to stay that way. She had the test done to determine if the type of cancer she had is genetic, and it is not. That does not mean that any of us will not develop the disease, but it does ease our mind a little.

Funny thing about our hair, she has yet to let her hair grow back long. Not because it can't, but because she found she loves the short afro style. She calls it, her get up and go hair. Her husband now keeps it trim and neat for her. I told her it was just hair. As India Arie says, "I am not my hair."

**THERE IS NO FORCE MORE POWERFUL THAN
A WOMAN DETERMINED TO RISE.**

SINEIDRA UNIQUE

HAVE MERCY ON ME, LORD, FOR I AM FAINT.
HEAL ME, LORD, FOR MY BONES ARE IN AGONY.
3MY SOUL IS IN DEEP ANGUISH. HOW LONG, LORD,
HOW LONG?

PSALMS 6:2

MY CANCER SCARE

In 1989, I started having some severe stomach cramps, and my cycle was unbearable. I would go to the doctor, and my pap came back abnormal. So here we go trying to figure out what was going wrong. I had a DNC done scraping out my uterus but still abnormal pap and horrible pain. When I say severe pain, I am talking about pain that would take you down to your knees. I remember crying and crawling to the bathroom at work one time because I was in so much pain. I was passing blood clots the size of your fist and would soak up a tampon and maxi pad in less than an hour. My normal cycle would last seven days, but now I was going ten to fourteen days, but the cramps would start at least a week earlier. I had severe headaches, and the doctor said it was because I was so anemic. One doctor would send me to another physician; that doctor would send me to a different doctor. My insurance would cover one doctor, but not the next. I was going through it to the fullest, but I still had two children that had to eat and live, so I had to go to work and make a living for them. I can say that my job was very supportive and helpful to me through this time, and I felt they had my back.

With all the doctor's visits and different times, I had to be off work, they never said anything to me.

I had one visit, where the technicians strapped me on a table, put this dye in my vajayjay and turned me upside down. They said they wanted to see where the dye was going too. I had a biopsy done of my uterus. Wait just one minute; you want to do what with what? They took a pair of tweezers the length of my arm and plucked tissue from my uterus for samples for testing. I even had to have tests done while I was on my cycle. Now that was the most disgusting thing ever. My mom was like are you pregnant in your tubes? You could imagine the looks I would give her. Pregnant hell no. I cannot even have sex; it hurts too much. Why every time something goes wrong down there, she thinks I am pregnant? I already have two kids, and I am not with their father now, why would I want another child. When I had the DNC, she said I was just having an abortion. At this moment, I felt like if having a child would take the pain away, let's do it.

Finally, my doctor suggests that I see this specialist in Carrollton, Georgia. Dr. Colditz. He specializes in OBGYN, and he was testing this new procedure out. Dr. Colditz was so backed up that he was not taking on new patients, but my doctor talked him into seeing me. When I went to Dr. Colditz, he told me that he had studied my case, and I had some options for relieving the pain. He said that they had found cancer cells growing in my uterus, but they could not be sure how fast the cells were growing until they went in. So, my options were to do chemo and kill cancer, they could go in and remove the area affected and around the cells, or we could do a hysterectomy. The first two options were maybe a fifty percent chance of getting everything, but with the hysterectomy, I had a ninety-eight percent chance of getting everything. Dr. Colditz says since I am so young and divorced, I might want to have more children one day, so he suggested the chemo and radiation. I remembered everything that my aunt went through, and that was not an option for me. I made my decision, and that was the hysterectomy. I told the doctor that I already have one girl and one boy, and if I decided to get married again, the person that I married would have to understand that I could not have any more children. I had to worry about raising the two children that I have; I could not worry about the children that had not even been planned to be around. We discussed my decision further, and I finally told that man, if you do not take this shit out of me, I do not care you could even hang a dick on me, I was done with this. He laughed but agreed to do the surgery. What kind of decision was that? I did not want to think about not being with my children, not seeing them graduate or have a family of their own. However, now I had to tell my mother what was happening? She just lost her baby sister a couple of years ago.

After my doctor's visit, I went back to work, and I was down. I had been crying, but I needed to go to work. Some idiot said something to me like at least you do not have cancer, and I broke down and cried. I just walked out and left. Well, the other manager at the restaurant, had no idea where I went, and if I was okay, so she called my mother to check on me. My mom had picked up my kids from daycare so that I could go to the doctor. I still had not figured out how to tell her what was going on, but I did not have to worry about that, because when the manager called my mother, she told her what the doctor had said. So, when I walked in my mom's house, she and my brother were there crying like someone had died. So here I go again. I told them what the game plan was, and I felt that I would be all right.

I prayed to God, to please heal me. "Lord, you know that I am a single mother, my children need me. Please if you will see fit to let me be alright, I promise to live better, to be a better mother, a better daughter, a better sister. Please, Lord, I need to be there for my children. Please let me live long enough to see my kids grow up. Please let them be old enough to be productive adults and can take care of themselves. In Your Darling Son Jesus Name, I pray." I prayed and prayed and prayed.

My surgery was scheduled for June 4th of 1990. I was going to be only the second person in Carrollton, Georgia to have a vaginal hysterectomy. I was not going to be cut, and they would remove everything other than one ovary. I had gone through months of treatment and trying different things to come to this day. Two days before my surgery was scheduled, I had to go to the hospital to give my own blood. You see, I have this very rare type of blood and in the case of an emergency and to be on the safe side, I had to donate my own blood to the hospital. I also had been advised to go to the financial department because there was something about my insurance policy that needed to be addressed. When I went in, they told me I had to pay my twenty percent for the surgery before it took place. I had to what? What's the cost of surgery? I laughed at them. I have insurance, and the insurance is covering 80% of the hospital bill, so what are you talking about? This very lovely older lady proceeds to tell me, that because they had no way of telling if I was going to survive I had to pay the projected balance of the surgery before they would do the surgery. I never had in my life heard of anything like that before. If I died, my life insurance would and could pay you off. She tells me that since I was having this new and rare procedure by having a vaginal hysterectomy, the balance had to be paid first. Don't you think you could have told me this before now? So, I continued to laugh and went home. I told them to cancel the surgery, and I would just go ahead and die.

My mom came to pick up my kids, and I told her the surgery was off. She could not understand what I was saying about paying the hospital bill first, so she said get in the car. We drove to Tanner Medical Center in Carrollton, and she walked into the finance department, spoke with the same lady I had talked to earlier and after a few choice words, my mom slammed a check on her desk and said now do the damn surgery. My mom just pulled the trump card. The surgery was back on as scheduled.

At five in the morning of June 4th, my sister drove me to the hospital. I did all the pre-op procedures, and I was ready to go down in history. My doctor comes in to check on me, and I was in excellent spirits. I was still laughing and talking, but nervous all the same. My mom was going to keep my daughter while I was in the hospital and my son went to stay with his dad and his other grandmother. He was only four years old, and he loved to jump and play. I thought that it was best if I didn't have to worry about him jumping on me after the surgery and hurting me. That was a big mistake, he cried to come home. He never spends the night away from home or me, other than with my mom while I work.

The nurses came in, and one gave me a pill that would start numbing me before they put the juice in my veins. I was off the chain with that little bitty pill. They rolled me into the operating room, and I was still wide awake. I was talking to everyone, but I was thinking, I am still wide awake here people. I had heard of people being put under, but not out, they could still see, hear and feel everything that was going on. I did not want that to be me. I had pap smears before, and the stirrups that they put your feet in was ordinary, but these stirrups were almost in the ceiling. I asked one of the nurses, who was supposed to put their feet in those. I did not think my legs were long enough to reach them, much less stay up there for the surgery. Everyone laughed, but I was serious. They reassured me that everything was going to be all right. A few minutes later, Dr. Colditz walks in, and he has another doctor with him. He introduces the other doctor to me and tells me that doctor was there in case of an emergency, and they had to open me up. What, is that what you tell your patient minutes before surgery? I guess, that little pill had me on a roll, so I asked him what kind of emergency and since he was the specialist, why did he need help? Again, everyone laughed, but again I was serious. I was talking to Dr. Colditz as he was putting on his gloves and scrubbing up, "Hey Doc, can you still hear me?" "Yes, Secelia, I hear you." "Well, Doc, I think that we have a problem." "Why do you say that?" "I still hear you, and you are ready to start." Laughter all around me again, why are these people laughing, this is a serious matter? Dr. Colditz walks over to me and looks at the anesthesiologist. He asked him if everything was okay and said let's begin. The anesthesiologist looks down at me and says he was about to cover my face with this mask, and he wanted me to count backward from one hundred. I nodded and started to count ninety-nine.

Mrs. Tolbert, Mrs. Tolbert, Mrs. Tolbert we need you to wake up now. Mrs. Tolbert, you need to wake up. Wake up, I just went to sleep, I'm only on ninety-eight. No Mrs. Tolbert, you must wake up. I was in recovery. I do not know what was in that mask, but it worked and worked fast. So now my mouth feels like someone stuck a nasty old tube sock down my throat and my gut is all wrapped up. I was not supposed to be cut, so why am I wrapped up like a mummy. I started coming out of my haze and asking questions. I'm hooked up to these machines, and people are fussing all over me. If you people would leave and turn off all these damn beepers, I could go back to sleep, and everything would be all right. But no such luck. Mrs. Tolbert, do you hear me? Yes, damn it, I hear you.

They move me to a room after a couple of hours in recovery, by this time I am in full blown out pain, and they have a morphine drip line hooked to me. I had this little button I could push when I was in pain. I would wake up and find more people in my room each time. By the time, the surgery was over, and I came to a room, my mother, grandmother, sister and father had all come to my hospital room. I was in a hospital gown, and that is all. I remember one time my grandmother said, "Oh Lord, she is showing us all of her backside" and my sister pulled the sheets back over my ass. I remember thinking that is what she gets for calling me a slut. I was waking up every fifteen minutes in pain and had to push my little button of morphine. My sister loved me so much that she started pushing the button for me every twelve to thirteen minutes. She had timed how often I was waking up, so she was helping me not to be in pain. A nurse came in and caught her and almost had a heart attack. She screamed at my sister and said that I had to do it because they did not want me to overdose on the morphine. My sister tried to explain her logic to the nurse, but she wasn't having none of that. I had to give myself the drugs. Okay, give me my button back. Evidently, I could cut back on the morphine the pain was getting better.

The doctor came in to see me earlier the next morning and told me that they had removed all the growth with the surgery. He said that I had made the best decision to have the surgery, because after they took out my uterus they could tell that the cancer was spreading and had already eaten a whole in my uterus. If I had not had the surgery, the disease would have spread to other organs and parts of my body. He also said since they had gotten everything, I did not need any other treatment, no radiation, and no chemo. My mother was like you did not have cancer because she never heard of anyone having cancer that didn't need chemo. Okay, mamma whatever? Dr. Colditz stood in the room and told her that I had cancer of the cervix, but they removed everything, and no further treatment would be needed. I had to stay in the hospital for a couple of more days, but I could go home and LIVE.

You know how God will play tricks on you and laugh at you. I was fine from cervical cancer, but in 2011, I found a mass in my left breast. How was I going to go through this again? I knew this was it because I had prayed and asked God before to let me live at least long enough to see my children grow up. By 2011, Mike had been in the league three years, and April had graduated from college and working as a General Manager in a restaurant. They both were very productive and living comfortable lives. I only could laugh because I was like okay God, you got jokes.

The doctor removed the mass as an outpatient surgery, but during the surgery, she found a cluster of tumors that she felt she needed to remove. A couple of weeks later, I went to the surgical center and had the benign mass removed. My sister kidnapped me. She would not let me drive to her house or even let my daughter drive me to the surgery. She picked me up and drove me. After the surgery, she drove me to her house and said I could not go home until she felt I was okay. I told her the doctor said, I could drive within twenty-four hours, and I could go home. They just wanted to make sure someone was with me the first night. My sister was having none of that. She finally said, "let me do this for me. I need to know you are okay." So, I shut up and went with her. It was not like I had a choice.

Secelia Tolbert

ACCEPT WHAT IS,

LET GO OF WHAT WAS,

AND

HAVE FAITH IN WHAT WILL BE

LESSONS LEARNED IN LIFE.COM

THE PERSON YOU TOOK FOR GRANTED TODAY, MAY TURN OUT TO BE THE PERSON YOU NEED TOMORROW. BE CAREFUL HOW YOU TREAT PEOPLE.

UNKNOWN

MAMA

Remember that I said that my mom pulled the trump card and paid my portion of the surgery that I would have had to pay for so I could have the surgery. Well, what I did not say was that I now owed my mother for the funds she so graciously came out of her pocket with. Once I returned to work and started receiving my quarterly bonus checks, I had to start making payments out of those bonus checks. That went on until I became a District Manager years later. I finally just said mama how much do I owe you? How much for the used sofa, that I got from you? How much for the dining room suite that you no longer had room for? How much for the use of your gas card (that I paid the monthly bill)? How much, how much? She gave me a total of $5,000.00. Really $5,000.00? I had been paying on this bill since 1990, and it is now 2004, and I still owe $5,000.00. I said okay, but things would have to be different. No longer would she control my bonus checks, no longer would she just come out of the blue and give me a dollar amount of how much I owed her. I was furious, but if I was in debt to her, I had no choice but to pay her back. I did not have any receipts or a record of how much I had paid her, and I was the one that came up with the idea, and I was going to live by it. I remember finding out that she was lying to me about a bill that I had in her name. When I first started driving and got my first car, she gave me a Chevron credit card. The card was in her name, and I could use it if I needed gas or anything for my car and did not have cash on hand. I continued to use the card for I guess twenty years or more, but I paid the bill. When the bill came in the mail, she would call me and tell how much I owed. I would send her a check or give her cash when I would see her. I never questioned her about the amount, but I never could seem to pay the card off. She would say you can't keep charging and expect to pay it off. I knew that, but I wasn't using it that much. One day in 2004 a very good friend of mine and I was talking about the Chevron card and a dining room suit that I bought from her in 1992. She wanted $1500.00 for the suit, and I had been paying her from bonus checks for the suit, and I could not get the damn thing paid off to save my life. Well, my friend suggested that I get the bill to come to my house instead of my mothers, but I could not do that legally since it was her bill. Then we decided to register the card online and then I would, at least, be able to see the bill. When my mother called to tell me the payment amount, I would already know the number. The problem was that she would say one thing, but the total to pay would be another. She was getting me anywhere from $25.00 to $50.00 every month. This went on for at least a year without her knowing that I knew the truth. It all came to blow one day when my daughter was going to see her grandmother, so I asked her to take the payment with her for me. I asked my daughter to call her Nanny and ask how much I owed, and I would send it to her. My daughter did not know that I had done this either, but when she came to pick up the money, I showed her the actual bill online, and she couldn't believe that Nanny would do something like that. When she gave mama the money, she also told her that I had the account online and knew how much the actual amount to pay. She was furious, why had I not told her I had the account online? How long have I been receiving the bill? I told her the truth, and she was pissed. Until I came up with the payment plan between the two of us, she would just call and say the Chevron bill is due.

119

Secelia Tolbert

The payment plan was to pay her $100.00 per month, with my bi-weekly paychecks. At this timed I, had begun to receive bonus checks from all three of my restaurants, so they were pretty nice. Even though I had to pay two rents, two cell phone bills and utilities for two locations, my income was now where I could live comfortably. I would make the monthly payments, and quarterly I would pay her a percentage of my bonus. This would mean that I would pay her $1,200.00 a year plus a percentage of my bonus. This plan would help me to pay off the debt within a couple of years. The problem came when she wanted to get more money from me from my bonus check than the percentage that we agreed. I would not give her any more than what was agreed upon. Within two years, I had paid her back in full. I kept receipts and had a log book where I would keep up with what happened when I paid her. Because for some reason, if I gave her cash, she would forget that I gave it to her and argued with me about making my payments. The day I paid her off, my sister, my mom and I were getting ready to head to Florida to one of my cousin's weddings. We sat at my sister's kitchen counter, and I counted out the balance in full. My sister stood right there and watched me count the money out to our mother. I even gave my mom a receipt that said PAID IN FULL. By the time, I received my next bonus check, my mom was asking where her money was.

We argued about the money, and I told her that I did not owe her anything. I reminded her that the total had been paid off, and I was no longer in debt to her. I asked her if she needed some money, I would help, but I did not owe her anything. She yelled at me and said she did not need my GD money or help; she wanted her money that I owed her. Well, we know how that went. I then found out that I did not raise my kids, she did. I found out that I never was a good mother, that she previously had turned me into the Department of Family & Children Services for being an unfit mother. What the HELL? My own mother had tried to take my children away from me. We did not actually speak to each other for almost three years after that. She would call to check on the kids, I would call to check on her, but neither one of us talked to each other. No matter what happened, I loved my mother, and I knew she loved me, but the relationship would never be the same.

It took some years, for me to learn that my mom loved me. Yes, I knew she loved me, but to know it deep down in my soul was something different. My mom's health had started failing, and she was having difficulty breathing. Her heart beat was irregular which was making it hard for her to walk and sometimes to even talk. She was having so many other problems with her body that she would say, getting old was just an inconvenience. You work all of your life to be able to live comfortable once you get old and retire, but once you retire you just don't feel like doing anything.

By this time, I had quit working, and I could go to her doctor's visits with her. We would have an appointment with the foot doctor on one day and the heart doctor the next. One week we would have to go see a doctor about a tumor they found in her head. The next week we would go see the doctor about her hip. Each physician gave her a different medicine to take. One of her prescriptions she had to take once a week on the same day and time. Now how was she supposed to remember that? I would set my alarm on my cell phone to remind me. The day before, I would remind her that she had to take the pill tomorrow. On the day of, I would call and five minutes before I would call. We visited each doctor's office with an insulated lunch box full of pill bottles. Before I started going with her, she would take all her medicine in a plastic grocery bag. I bought the lunch box and put her medicine in it for more convenience. I would drop her off at the front door. After parking the car, I could throw the strap over my shoulder, grab both of our purses and high tail it into the office before they called her back to a patient room.

In 2008, she had to have her hip replaced, but due to her heart, they could not put her to sleep. They numbed the area, but she still could see and hear everything that was going on in the operating room. She said she could not feel anything but pressure from the doctor performing the surgery. She remembered them using something like a sledgehammer to knock her replacement joint into place. She was a trooper. I could be there for her recovery, and I think this was when she started seeing me in a different light. At the hospital, the three of us was there, but I was not working so it only made sense that I stayed overnight or come early in the morning. She would only be there for a short period, and my brother had moved back home with her so he would be with her at the house when she came home. I left the hospital to go to the house to take a shower, and she was in one room, but when I returned a couple of hours later, they had moved her to another room. When I walked into that empty room with a custodian cleaning it, I was about to panic. Where was my mom, she was fine when I left? A nurse came and told me, they moved her to a different room, she was all right.

I went upstairs to the new room and was pissed off. I walked in that room, and my mother was crying. She was in so much pain from the move upstairs, and her nurse had not come back to give her any pain medication. She also was having difficulty breathing because she needed to be elevated or, at least, have two pillows to hold her head up. They did not want to raise the bed because of her surgery, and the nurse was supposed to be bringing her another pillow. My brother was with her, and when he saw me, he said oh shit. I was confused, what'cha mean oh shit? He had told them I was coming back and they had better take care of my mom before I got back.

I went to the nurse's station and asked for the supervisor. They informed me that they would get my mother's nurse. Obviously, she was too busy, since she had not come back to the room, so I did not need to see her. The floor nurse spoke with me, and I informed her that I walked into my mother's room, and she was crying because she was in so much pain. How could that be? She apologized and said she would take care of it. We had a few more words (I will not say which ones, but I did not curse) and my mom was taken care of for the remainder of her stay. When three nurses rushed into my mother's room, my brother laughed at them saying, "I told you my sister was coming back." I still don't understand that, but I came back.

In 2009, her heart was getting worse and with the lovely insurance companies and their policies, she was jumping hoop after hoop to get something done. Her doctor said she needed a defibrillator to regulate her heart rate. However, to have the device implanted in her heart, she would have to go through a cardioversion first. The procedure was done and was supposed to be an outpatient procedure. My uncle, aunt, and I sat in the waiting room while the doctors performed the cardioversion on my mama. My sister and brother did not come because this was supposed to be a simple in and out procedure. The doctor came out to speak to us and said as soon as he performed the cardioversion on my mama, her heart jumped right back out of rhythm, and the procedure had made her heart work harder, so they have decided to keep her overnight. After a few hours in recovery, they moved her to a room on the heart floor. I had the task of calling my children, my sister, and my brother. I spoke with each of them while my mother slept and labored to breathe. I was looking at her and watching how hard it was for her to breath, and I knew that she would not be with us much longer.

We stayed in the hospital for a week until my mom could be released. On the way from the hospital, we had to stop and pick up her new medication. I ran into the pharmacy while my mother and cousin waited in the car. My mom opened up to my cousin and told her that I was a decent person. She told my cousin that she knew that I loved her and would always do anything and everything to make sure she and my family was okay. The conversation went on about how she has always loved me, but I was so stubborn that it was sometimes hard to get along with me, but she knows that she raised me that way. She told my cousin that I was a hard worker and how proud of me she was. I understand now that she used my cousin as a messenger, she knew that Tonya would tell me everything that she said. But I realized that she relied on me when we went to the hospital to do her pre-op. The morning before the cardioversion, we went to the hospital to do the standard pre-op that all patients must do before having any procedure done in a hospital. Going over all her emergency contact information, the assistant turned a second computer monitor around for us to view the information as she went over what my mom had said. Next of kin, IS THAT MY NAME AND NUMBER AND NOT MY SISTER? Yep, my mom, had given the hospital and her doctor's office my name and number as the person to contact in case of an emergency. I was surprised, when did she do this? Just two weeks prior the last doctor's visit, my sister was that person and every other doctor or lawyer office, my sister was the emergency contact person. I knew then that she just had given the information within a couple of days because I got a new cell phone number maybe two days before. Which means she had to call and give the new number to the hospital, I mattered to her. Maybe I sound crazy, but I mattered to her, and it felt good.

Instead of going home she went to my sister's house because my townhouse had too many stairs for her to go up and down. Before she left the hospital, her doctor told her that they would have to retry the cardioversion again before her insurance would agree to pay for an implanted defibrillator. One thing for sure is that she definitely did not want to go through with the procedure again. She said it was like getting kicked from the front and back by a bull at the same time. She had burns on her thighs and on her back from the procedure. That was how powerful the shock waves were from the cardioverter. The first procedure was done in October, and she was scheduled to have the second procedure done December 1st.

Thanksgiving of 2009, my mom sat at the table and told my sister, brother, and daughter how she wanted to be buried. I was in San Diego with Mike for Thanksgiving so he would not be alone.   She told them who she wanted to conduct her ceremony and what songs she wanted to be played. She wanted to be laid to rest next to her baby sister. She even told them where her clothes were that she wanted have put on her. They joked not taking her serious, my sister telling her, "you'll be dead, I can do what I want." My mom responded and said I'll come back and haunt you too. No one thought anything else about that conversation on Monday, November 30th when my mom passed from congestive heart failure. She had died one day before her next cardioversion procedure was supposed to be done.

That Monday morning, I arrived back in Atlanta after my trip to San Diego and like every other time that I traveled, I called to inform my mama that I was back. When I would get back to my car, if I didn't call her and let her know that I was back and safe she would fuss with me, so I called just as I was supposed to. We talked about the game over the weekend. We discussed Mike's girlfriend Shianette and how much in love Mike was with her. Mama said I'll never get to meet her, and I said mama you know Mike will bring her home when the season is over. "No baby, I'll never get to meet her." I thought that she knew she could not fly anymore because of her heart. She was laughing and talking about the things that she and her best friend had been doing. We use to call them Thelma and Louise. The two of them would go find trouble. They once went to see what was going on in a hostage situation. Martha-Nell had this old beat-up pickup truck, and the two went everywhere together.

Mama had started walking with a cane, not for her knees or legs but for her heart. She used the cane to hold her up. She had got to the point where she could hardly walk to the bathroom down the hall in her own house. On that Monday, Martha-Nell, and mama went to two different doctor visits as they both had to go to the doctor. They went to the bent can store and to the grocery store. Martha-Nell said that mama did not use her cane at all that day, that she was doing good. Mama was getting in and out of the truck without any problems. They had a great day. After Martha-Nell had dropped my mama off that evening, the pickup truck got stuck in the mud in front of my mama's house. So, my mama drove her home and came back to the house to cook dinner for her and my brother.

Secelia Tolbert

She talked to my sister and then called my brother around 7:00 that evening. She told him she was getting ready to put dinner on and wanted to know what time he would be home. He explained that he was already off work, but he had to drop my cousin off, and he would be home around 7:30. He walked in to a house full of smoke. He yelled out her name, and she didn't answer. He thought she must be in the back and didn't realize that the food was burning up. He walked to the back of the house and checked her bedroom, the bathroom, and the spare bedroom. She was nowhere to be found. He came back to the kitchen and took the pot of peas off the stove and decided to take the pot outside because it was so badly burned.

As he walked back into the house, he noticed my mother laying on the daybed in the family room. My brother was a safety coordinator for the company that he worked for and is a trained in CPR procedures. He tried to revive her until the First Responders arrived and took over. They took her to the hospital and continued trying to revive her, but God had other plans. My brother had called my cousin to come up there, and the phone calls started. The amazing thing that happened to me that night, around 7:15 that evening as I was sitting on my couch and watching TV, some sixty miles away, I got the cold chill to rush through my body, and I thought what in the world was that. I have never experienced a feeling like that before nor have I since that moment. About thirty minutes after the chill, I received the call from my cousin telling me to come to the hospital that mama was sick. I knew in my heart; my mom was gone. I kept asking my cousin what was going on, but he kept trying to tell me she was okay, just come to the hospital. I told him to put my brother on the phone, but he said he couldn't talk to me at that moment. I knew for sure then. Just tell me the truth, I asked him and he did. He said that Tony found her when he got home and tried to revive her, but it was too late.

I made my round of calls after I yelled out in grief. My daughter came to get me, and we made that long ride to the hospital just to say goodbye to the woman that gave me life. My sister and her husband had made it there before I did, but no one told her that mama was gone. She didn't find out until she got to the hospital, so when I walked in she was just finding out. I had a few minutes to get myself together before I arrived at the hospital, but my sister was going through the initial phase of finding out that Mama did not make it. I was told that mama was still in the emergency room, and they had not cleaned her up yet. It didn't matter to me, I needed to see my mama. The nurses advised me against going in the room, but nothing was going to stop me from walking in that room at that moment.

I never expected to see what I saw as I walked through those doors. My mom had this glow all over her. She seemed to be smiling. Her clothes were ripped, her hair was a mess, but she was smiling. The smile looked as it was coming from deep down in her soul. She was at peace, and you could tell that she was happy at last. I talked to her for a while and then I kissed her on her forehead and said, "I love you, rest in peace now." I told her to find Aunt Helen and Granddaddy and laugh. You've made it now, it's done. And then I laughed and said, "you really meant you were not going to have another cardioversion done."

We buried my mama on Friday, December 4th at her church and laid her to rest next to her baby sister. The ceremony went as she wished, we did not want her to come back and haunt us, so we did as we were told. The only wish that we did not do was bury her in the outfit that she suggested. The funeral director, also our cousin, informed us that the outfit was too worn out or old or something I really don't remember, that week went by so fast. But we ended up getting something else for her to wear. My sister and I bought matching scarfs to wear one that matched the scarf that we had put on our mother. We also bought our brother a tie to match. All her grandchildren and great-grandkids wore the same color.

When we drove up to the church, there were miles and miles of cars. People came to pay their last respects to our mother. That was a peaceful experience because so many people loved her. We were told that if we had held the service on that Saturday, there would have been double the amount of people there. We did the service on Friday so Mike could get home for the service, he would have to fly out to Cincinnati on Saturday morning to play with the Chargers.

When he first got home, we went to see her before the service, and he introduced Shianette to his Nanny. He told her, he was bringing Shianette to meet her in January, but she did hang around. He let her know that Shianette was the one. After the service, the family was going back to mama's house to gather together, but Mike said he couldn't handle all the people. People were more concerned about him being in the league than the fact that his grandmother was just buried. So, he said he was going to do a little retail therapy. We went to the mall and went shopping. I had a cousin to tell me that I was not grieving right because I was not crying like everyone else. I tried to remind her that I was the one that had been with mama through all the doctors' visits. I was the one at the hospital for the cardioversion. I was the one that saw her right after she passed in the emergency room. I knew in my heart of hearts that my mama was alright. I knew the smile on her face as she laid in the hospital and the glow that was all over her was a smile saying I am happy. I am alright. I am IN THE PRESENCE OF THE LORD. So instead of us being sad and mourning her death, we should be rejoicing her new life.

Do I miss her, yes indeed? Even with all the years of not getting along, I miss her terribly. I talked to her every day, and I ask her for her opinion. Funny, I did not want her advice when she was alive, but now I ask what she thinks about everything that I do. My mother was a hard worker, a loyal friend, but most of all she was a great mother.

WE ALL HAVE GONE THRU,

BUT HE WALKS WITH ME &

HE TALKS WITH ME.

Secelia Tolbert

THERE CAN BE NO GROWTH

WITHOUT PERSONAL DEVELOPMENT

YOU WERE CREATED TO MAKE

SOMEBODY ELSE LIFE

BETTER.

SOMEBODY NEEDS:

 WHAT YOU HAVE,

YOUR SMILE,

YOUR LOVE,

YOUR WORDS &

YOUR ENCOURAGEMENT.

REALIZATION OF A DREAM

Before April turned one year old, she was walking and talking. At fifteen months she was potty trained. She started bringing me her dirty diaper, no matter what was in the diaper, so I had to potty train her quickly. By the age of two, she could hold a complete, understandable conversation with anyone. She had a memory like an elephant, she remembered everything. At the age of four, she was evaluated and found to be a genius. She has saved my life more than once. She is my quiet child. I call her my career student for she has four degrees, a specialist certificate, and now is working on her Master's Degree. At the age of sixteen, she was a shift manager for me at the restaurant I worked. She became a General Manager before the age of twenty-two. She is the smartest person I know. Her brain never stops analyzing and inquiring about life itself. She can debate with the best of them. She is stubborn and will not take any mess from anyone (I wonder where she got that from). Yet, she is still silent, but I think that is because she is sitting back, watching and learning.

Now Mike, like his sister is very smart, but sometimes he will let life get in the way. Energetic is not the word you should use when describing my bubbling baby boy. Never actually crawling, Mike went from scooting across the floor on one knee to running. Keeping up with him was a full-time job. When he was younger, I bought the child harness that you could attach to his wrist to keep up with him. The problem with the device was that he would just take it off and would be gone. I would feel the slack in the line and knew he was gone. He was so fast, I would have to drop everything to find him. Once my mom was taking the grandkids to Six Flags, and I told her to make sure she got the harness. She called it a leash and she would not put her grandchild on a leash. I tried to explain that it was for his safety and her sanity, but no she would not take it. Hours after searching and crying because she had lost my baby at Six Flags, an employee took her to "Lost Parents." She walked in the little cottage, and finds my son saying "Nanny, you lost me." From that moment on, she never left the house without making sure the harness was in the bag.

As a single parent, I had to work. Sometimes two or three jobs at once. Finding daycare and nightmare for my babies, was an adventure at least. I was fortunate enough to make my own work schedule, giving me the flexibility to work around game and practice schedules. I thank God each and every day for the children that he gave me. I could work without worrying about them. They were self-sufficient and responsible. Never mind about the woods catching fire in the back yard or the boy that needed fourteen stitches after he tried to break in, I did not have to worry.

I don't think I did anything special or different from any other single parent. I was a no-nonsense mother. I did not have time for foolishness. They had one job, and that was to get good grades. Nothing else came before that. Knowing that April was so smart, I was concerned when Mike was getting ready to start school. In my mind, I knew his teachers were going to have a hand full with him. He was so, so Michael. Yes, he was smart, but he had other stuff on his mind. He surprised me. His kindergarten teacher called him her sponge. He could remember everything. He could tell her what she was wearing on any day. He finished his work before everyone else and would help other students with their work. The problem with that is that, once he finished he was ready to do something else. So the teachers had to learn to give him extra work or he would be bothering the other kids.

Both of my babies received awards for intelligence; President Scholars, Superintendent Scholars, Who's Who Among (This and That), you name it, they received it. But they both wanted to play sports as well. Basketball, football, baseball, and track here we come. Our life changed as we became more and more involved with the different sports. You can participate in anything you want to, but you have to complete the season after I pay the registration fees was my rule. I'm sorry if you decided you didn't want to do it, it's a done deal. If my job was work and figure out all the extra money, your job is to keep your grades up and stay out of trouble. We had a great little system going for our little family of three.

Years and years of time and money put into my children sports life. I became Team Mom, a member of different Boards of Directors, I even coached the boys and girls basketball teams for about three years, I fed every football player on every team in high school on Thursdays during the season for three years. And, I only missed one game of either one of my kids in twelve years. If there was any doubt, yes, I am that mother that could yell louder than anyone else in the stands. I am probably the only parent to receive a technical foul while sitting at the scorer's table. The things that I did, never in my mind did I do it for future repayment. I loved each and every minute that it took for my children to be involved. Sports was just another way to keep their minds from idling and figuring out ways to do the wrong thing.

April chose to stop playing organized school sports and play recreational basketball in high school. She created a program for her high school that would bridge students together. The idea of the program was that incoming freshmen were afraid and lost in the huge high school, upperclassmen would become mentors for the freshmen giving them advice and directions. The program is now recognized in all five county high schools and is called Bridges. After graduation, she attended Georgia State University and is now the Human Resource Generalist for my city.

Mike, on the other hand, made sports his goal. He is competitive by nature and will challenge anyone, in almost any sport. Bowling, swimming, golfing, wrestling, weight lifting and boxing are just a few sports that he loves and do well other than football. He still holds a record for hitting the longest homerun at a local park, and he set that record when he was nine. He was always one of the best players on any team, but what makes him stand out from other players is that he is so smart. He is able to learn the plays not only for his position but every position on the field. When I was coaching him in basketball, he could tell each player where they were supposed to be doing. I called him my coach on the court. His coaches throughout the years have always said that he would make it. Not only because of his talent but his attitude and his dedication to his craft.

To be a parent, not just a single parent, and to witness the success of a child is an unexplainable feeling, but to have two children that are successful as a single mother is undeniably the greatest feeling in the world. No one could say anything negative to me because I am on top of the world. In high school and college, Mike's desire and will to become the best skyrocketed. He trained harder than anyone I know. He would be the first person to arrive and sometimes the last to leave, he went in on Sundays to watch film with the coaches. So many people had told him he would not make it. Either he was too short for a position, or too big for others. He was once told by an NFL Scout that he would never make it in the NFL, we see how that went. Coach David Bennett bought a helmet of that team and put it in Mike's locker and then told him that was his inspiration to make it. He had to prove himself all the time, so now before every game, I tell him, "Show the world what I've always known."

San Diego Chargers and Coach Norv Turner gave him that chance and he ran with it. One early morning for me and late night for him (3-hour time difference), Mike called and said, "Mama, I made it!" I could tell he was emotional, so I sat up and talked to him. He continued to say, "you know how many people want to be here where I'm at. How many college players that tried out and wanted to make it to the NFL, but God saw fit to let me make it." I asked what was he doing, and he states that he was just sitting outside looking up at the stars and thanking God for his blessings. He finally realized that everything that he had done, everything that he/we sacrificed was for this very moment. He said, "now is the time for the real work to begin." I understood his thought because just as bad as he wanted to be there, there are thousands of other players wanted to be there also. He had to put the work in to keep his position and to continue to play in the NFL.

Did I know that he was going to become one of the best fullbacks in the NFL? No, but did I believe that he could be the best fullback in the NFL? Yes. He can do and be the best at anything that he puts his mind too. I knew he had it in him, but as we all know, this life can be hard and cruel. All we needed was for someone to give him a chance. I have been asked I know at least one hundred times, "How do I feel about having my son play in the Super Bowl?" And my answer now and then has been the same;

HOW DO I FEEL? MY SON PLAYED IN THE SUPER BOWL. THAT'S HOW I FEEL!!!! MY SON, THAT I RAISED ALONE. MY SON THAT HAS TO DEAL WITH MORE THAN MOST BOYS GROWING UP. MY SON, THAT TURNED OUT TO BE THE BEST HUSBAND, FATHER, SON, BROTHER, FRIEND THAT ANYONE COULD EVER ASK FOR. MY SON THAT DESERVES ALL THAT GOD HAS BLESSED HIM WITH. PLAYED IN THE SUPER BOWL. HIS DREAM CAME TRUE, THEREFORE MY DREAM CAME TRUE!

MY SON PLAYED IN THE SUPER BOWL!

SOME PEOPLE WANT IT TO HAPPEN...

SOME WISH IT WOULD HAPPEN...

OTHERS MAKE IT HAPPEN...

IT ONLY TAKES ONE PERSON TO CHANGE YOUR

LIFE....

YOU!!!!

MY ADVICE TO YOU

Understand, this is my opinion and my opinion only. I did the best that I could to raise both of my children. I do not have a Philosophy Degree nor have I studied children behaviors. I am just merely a mother that loves her children. I am just a woman that cares about what is happening to our youth of today's society. I honestly know that there are no two children that are alike, but I do know that if we as parents do not step in and take back our kids we will be looking for a world of trouble. I am a firm believer that God has our back, and He is always there for us. No matter if you are religious are not, it is your job to raise your children. The dynamic of families has changed so much over the years, we have grandparents raising grandchildren. Great-grandparents stepping in to provide for their grandchildren's children. Uncle, aunts, and strangers raising out children. Please stop the madness!

First and foremost, remember that God gave our children to us as gifts. They are not ours to keep. We are to love and nourish them. We are to feed, clothe, give shelter, but mostly love them. Not one of them asked to be here, but God makes no mistakes. So, if your child wasn't planned by you, know your child was planned. We will get tired, we will want to give up, but giving up is not an option.

Remember what the judge told my ex-husband when you eat, they need to eat. When you sleep, they need to have a pillow to lay their heads on. When you put on your shoes, they need shoes to wear too. Be there for them. Get to know them each individually. There are no two-people identical, even children. Learn their personalities, don't compare one to another. Find what makes them tick. Find their passion. What do they want to be when they grow up? What are their dreams for the future?

Support your children, do not be drop-off parents. Go to games or academic functions. Get to know their friends and their friend's families. Know who are children is hanging around. Set boundaries. Give them limits for everything. Talk to them and LISTEN to them. Remember, listening requires you to understand and hear what they are saying. I'm not saying you have to agree or do whatever but listen to them.

It is your responsibility to keep them safe. There is nothing wrong with you going into their rooms. Their rooms will tell you a lot about them, and if that room is in your house, you can go in. I'm not saying barge in and be nosey, however, if you see them changing and not their usual self, by all means be nosey. Let them know you care, children need discipline. They will love you for it in the long run.

STOP SPOILING THEM!!!!!!!!!!!!!!!!!!!!!!!!!! They do not have to have the best of everything. People take better care of things that work for and deserve. If they want that $300.00 pair Jordan's, they need to work and earn a part of the money, even if you can afford them. They don't have to have all the latest gadgets. They will be alright. They need to be responsible children before they can be responsible adults. Give them chores. Even at two years old, they can do chores. Clean-up clean-up, it's time to clean-up. As they get older, give them more to do. Their behavior can reward them things they want. Don't reward them for being bad. Don't negotiate with them.

Education is paramount. Make them understand that without an education, it will be hard for them to get anywhere in life. When applying for a job today, a high school diploma is almost like not having one at all. Organizations want someone that have attended some form of Secondary Institution. Whether a university, college, or technical, but if they don't have a high school diploma or GED, they cannot continue their education. We must push our children to break the chain. If you did not go to college, encourage your child to attend. If you did and, have your degree support your kids as they go.

Teach them to be respectful. They do not have to like anyone, but they damn sure need to respect people. Teach them to say yes ma'am and sir or no ma'am or sir. Teach them to address another adult by Ms. or Mr. A child calling an adult by their first name is entirely disrespectful. Teach them to be leaders and not followers. Teach them to stand up for what is right. But most of all teach them when it is best to give in and live to regroup to fight another day. Being the show for their friends is not cute and most of the times their friends are laughing at them and not with them.

Please teach them how to address. Ladies be the example of how you want your daughters to dress. Learn the difference of club clothes or bedroom clothes and school clothes. No wonder our young men are having trouble concentrating at school. I am not a fan of school uniforms, but when a girl can get on the bus with a slip on as a dress and go to school all day and not be sent home, then we need to consider school uniforms. Gentlemen, teach your young men how to tie a tie knot. Invest in some dress clothes that don't hang down their behinds. There is nothing wrong with having clothes like these, but there are a time and a place for everything. When kids are going to school like they just turned over and got on the bus, we need to address this problem. And know that it is not only the teachers and principal to check what your children are wearing, IT IS ALSO YOURS!

Raising children is a hard job, and they don't come with a how-to manual. It is hard for a mother and father as a team, but it is extremely hard for single parents. But it is possible to be done. WE ARE THEIR PARENTS FIRST AND FRIEND SECOND. No one said it was going to be easy, but nothing worth having ever is. Be kind, be strict, don't punish out of anger, and love on them. Kiss and hug on them even in public. Hold and comfort them when they cry, for they will. Laugh and celebrate their victories. Be their biggest cheerleader and supporter, but be the first to snap when they need it. Let them fear you. (lol). They need to fear you as you fear God.

Encourage them to bring God back into their lives. Praying at school can still be done, although silently, they can still pray. Encourage them to pray for their friends, their teachers, even the school building. Motivate them to pray before they take a test or play a game. Be the example that inspires them. When we know better, we will do better. Pray for and with each other.

Secelia Tolbert

BE PATIENT

EVERYTHING IS COMING

TOGETHER

FOR HIS GOOD!!!

ABOUT THE AUTHOR

Secelia Walker Tolbert, is the mother of two and grandmother of five. She now lives in a suburb of Atlanta, Georgia and works for the Douglas County School Board. Retiring from the fast food world after twenty-nine years, Secelia still operates a small catering company where she loves to cook for friends and family. Her specialties are cornbread dressing and banana pudding.

After dropping out of school in 1981, Secelia recently returned and graduated from Ashford University, Forbes School of Business. She promised her mother that she would someday return and finish her education, a promise that she finally kept. Receiving a Bachelor's Degree in Organizational Management with Specializations in Human Resource Management and Sports & Recreational Management, she plans to continue working with the school system and begin her next career as an author.

Recently, the Tolbert Family founded "The Tolbert Family S.P.A.D.E. Foundation where their objective is to help single parents and the development of education. As a single parent, Secelia knows the trials that single parents face daily and she is glad to be in the situation where she can give back and help the next person. As a Motivational Speaker, Secelia gives details on her life experiences and believes that if she can help just one person, she is carrying on what God has planned for her.